Communication Skills

Your Guide to Improving Social Intelligence, Developing Charisma, and Learning How to Talk to Anyone

By: Devin White

ALL RIGHTS RESERVED

No part of this book may be reproduced, stored in a retrieval system, or transmitted in any form or by any means, electronic, mechanical, photocopying, recording, scanning, or otherwise, without the prior written permission of the publisher.

Limit of Liability/Disclaimer of Warranty: the publisher and the author make no representations or warranties with respect to the accuracy or completeness of the contents of this work and specifically disclaim all warranties, including without limitation warranties of fitness for a particular purpose. No warranty may be created or extended by sales or promotional materials. The advice and strategies contained herein may not be suitable for every situation. This work is sold with the understanding that the publisher is not engaged in rendering medical, legal or other professional advice or services. If professional assistance is required, the services of a competent professional person should be sought. Neither the publisher nor the author shall be liable for damages arising herefrom. The fact that an individual, organization or website is referred to in this work as a citation and/or potential source of further information does not mean that the author or the publisher endorses the information the individuals, organization or website may provide or recommendations they/it may make. Further, readers should be aware that websites listed on this work may have changed or disappeared between when this work was written and when it is read.

Table of Contents

Introduction 1
   A Brief Walk Through History 1
   What Is Communication? 1
   Why Do We Communicate? 3
   The Communication Process 5
   Communication Principles 6

Chapter 1: Effective Communication 9
   What is Effective Communication? 9
   Principles of Effective Communication 13
   Verbal and Nonverbal Communication 14
   Verbal Communication 22
   Creating Persuasive and Memorable Messages 24
   Asking Thoughtful Questions 27
   Perceptions Versus Reality 30
   Effectiveness in Other Forms of Communication 34
   Conflict and Resolution 38
   Conflict Resolution 39
   Communicating Effectively with Technology 40

Chapter 2 Part 1: Constructive Communication 46
   What is Constructive Communication? 46
   What is Deconstructive Communication? 49

   Listening and Formulating Thoughts *54*

Chapter 2 Part 2: Emotions and their Role in Communication 60

   Regulation of Emotions *61*

Chapter 3 Part 1: The Importance of Listening 63

   Why is Listening Important? *63*

   The Listening Process *64*

Chapter 3 Part 2: Listening Types 68

   What are the Types of Listening? *68*

   The Challenge of Listening *73*

   What are Some of the Barriers to Listening? *75*

   Listening Practices that Affect Communication. *78*

   Types of Listening Responses *80*

Chapter 4: Emotions 85

   What are Emotions? *85*

   Elements of Emotions *85*

   Emotions and Communication *87*

   Purpose of Emotions *89*

   Role of Emotions *90*

   Four Ways to Improve Your Emotional Awareness *93*

   Guidelines for Expressing Emotions *94*

   Managing and Responding to Emotions *97*

Chapter 5: Dynamics of Interpersonal Relationships 99

   What is Interpersonal Communication? *99*

The Two Aspects of Interpersonal Communication............ 102

Conflict and Interpersonal Communication 104

Conflict Management Styles.. 105

Elements of the Five Strategies for Managing Conflict 106

Negotiation Steps... 109

Relational Dynamics and Communication 112

Knapp's Relationship Escalation Model 114

Knapp's Relationship Termination Model.......................... 116

Chapter 6: Important Communication Barriers/Mistakes/Obstacles 119

Common Barriers 119

Other Communication Barriers: 124

Communication Barriers We've Discussed Previously: 125

Organizational-Level Communication Barriers 126

Overcoming Barriers 130

Basic Communication Fixes... 132

How to Avoid and Fix Communication Breakdowns Within a Team 136

Chapter 7 Part 1: Improving Communication Skills 139

Top Communication Skills 140

What is Persuasion?... 143

How Does it Increase Our Communication Effectiveness? 144

Chapter 7 Part 2: How to Talk to Anyone 148

Communication Styles 148

- The Four Communication Styles: 149
- Understanding and Leveraging Motivations 159
- The Three Main Underlying Motivations 160
- Developing Social Intelligence 164
- How Can We Develop Social Intelligence? 167
- Audience Analysis 168
- Audience-Centered Approach to Communication 169
- Key Takeaways 172

Chapter 8: Powerful Presentation 174

- Broad Presentation Categories 174
- Why are Presentations Necessary? 175
- What are the Elements that Make a Bad Presentation? .. 177
- What are the Elements that Make a Good Presentation? 178
- Presentation Hesitation 179
- Acknowledge the Barriers 180
- How to Handle the Fear? 182
- Counter the Effects of our Fight-or-Flight Response 182
- Best Practices 184
- The EME 186
- The Introduction 193
- The Body 194
- The Conclusion 195
- Dynamic versus Static 196

Chapter 9 Part 1: Communication Strategies for a Virtual Age 199

> What is Virtual Communication? 199
>
> What are Some of the Advantages of Virtual Teams and Virtual Communication? 200
>
> What are Some of the Disadvantages of Virtual Teams and Virtual Communication? 203
>
> Communication Mistakes in Virtual Communication and In-person Communication 204
>
> What about Virtual Communication? 209
>
> Addressing Attribution Bias 213
>
> Strategies for Positive Difficult Conversations and How to Make People Feel Valued and Heard 217
>
> Effective and Impactful Meetings 220

Chapter 9 Part 2: What In-person Communication Principles and Techniques Can We Apply to Virtual Teams? 226

> What happens if the team is too unfamiliar with each other and the chatroom doesn't take off as it should? 228

Introduction

A Brief Walk Through History

Travel back in time some six million years. You'll find the earliest human ancestors communicating with grunts, signs, and gestures. Fast-forward a few million years and you'll find that communication had evolved to include smoke-signals, drums, whistles, and even cave paintings. It wasn't until about 150,000 years ago that man first started using language.

Even though communication in any of its several forms has been around since the dawn of humankind, we are yet to master its finer intricacies.

What Is Communication?

Communication happens when information is transferred from one person or group to another. It could be as straightforward as a sender passing a message to a recipient. For instance, a greeting by way of a nod between two people passing each other on the street, or a mother patting her child to comfort it. The sender (mother) is passing a message (pat) to the recipient (the child). The gentle, loving gesture reassures the child that everything will be alright.

Equally, communication could be complicated, involving several elements. Let's revisit the scenarios mentioned above.

> A greeting by way of a nod and a smile between two people passing each other on the street.
> A greeting by way of a nod and a frown between two people passing each other on the street.

As people, even strangers, can 'nod' at each other in passing, the act itself tells us very little. The addition of the smile or the frown gives us more insight. It clues us in to whether or not they like each other.

> A mother coos and pats her child to comfort it.
> A mother glances at the door frequently while patting her child to comfort it.

The first situation depicts a patient and compassionate mother, while the second scenario shows us a nervous or panicky mother.

While communication in itself is simple, several elements can lend baffling levels of complexity to communication. As an example, consider a judge delivering a verdict in a courtroom full of people. Are the people sitting rigidly, leaning forward in their seats, or jumping to their feet? Are they speaking in their normal tone, or are their voices hushed or raised? What do their facial expressions, hand gestures, or eye movements convey?

One of the first things that influence how communication is perceived is nonverbal cues. The way we sit or stand. Whether we are still or fidgeting, or are we facing the other person or not? All aspects of our body language and micro-expressions, right down to whether our pupils are dilated or not, the tone of our voice, even the way we dress, are considered nonverbal communication. Spoken or verbal is another form of communication that can carry as many clues as nonverbal; for instance, the words we choose or the emotion in our voice. The final two forms of communication—written and visualizations—carry as much weight and invoke equal amounts of complexity as nonverbal and verbal communications.

Why Do We Communicate?

We communicate every day, be it at home, at work, or in a public setting. Why? Because communication in any of its forms is crucial to achieving our goals. It's indispensable for forming and managing relationships. And without it, we cannot share ideas and affect progress.

What are some of the things we can accomplish through communication?

A child selling lemonade in front of their house, girl or boy scouts going door to door selling cookies, a politician running a campaign, a brand management team working with a company—these are all examples of persuasive communication. When we want others to do something we want or desire, we use this form of communication.

A hurricane, flood, or other disaster warnings, election results, budget announcements, or changes in tax filing—these are examples of information-based communication. When we want to tell others what to expect or what has changed, we use this communication form.

Using a GPS, doubt clarification at school or the workplace, inquiries into how things are done, tests in a laboratory, and calls to customer care centers, are all examples of information-seeking communication. When we have questions, or seek clarity or knowledge, we use this form of communication.

Crying or laughing, a brisk walk or a saunter, raised or soft tone of voice, finger-pointing or arms crossed in front or behind us—these are all examples of how we use emotion-filled communication. When we want to express our feelings, we tend to drop huge clues through emotion-rich body language.

The Communication Process

The communication process is simply the steps or actions involved in sending a successful communication. As before, this is an oversimplified explanation. Several steps are involved in the communication process, each possessing the power to cause confusion or misunderstandings.

In its simplest form, communication happens when a sender sends a message via a medium or communication channel to a receiver.

The mother from the earlier example used a pat as her communication channel to reassure her child. She would have considered several factors when she chose her medium. The child's age, for instance. The younger the child, the more likely that nonverbal communication would have a more significant impact. Their environment would be another influencing factor. If in a crowded public space with lots of noise, nonverbal communication would be easier to process than the mother being forced to speak loud enough to be heard while maintaining a soothing tone. Since speaking loudly is not associated with a state of calmness, in doing so, she would not elicit the correct response.

The process does not end with the message being sent or the selection of a medium. Once sent, the communication needs to be decoded by the recipient. The child would 'decode' a soft pat as a comforting gesture. However, a harder pat or frantic patting could be construed as punishment or impatience. This interpretation would then have the opposite effect on the child than intended by the mother.

Thus, the communication process requires both the sender and the receiver to minimize potential misunderstanding and understand the meaning and significance of nonverbal cues for effective communication to occur.

Feedback is another crucial component of an effective communication process. When a misunderstanding occurs, or there is a breakdown in the communication process, the receiver should seek clarification or engage in reflection to ensure that the message sent has been understood correctly. In this case, an increase in the intensity of the child's crying would be 'feedback' that the mother would use to make her communication more effective.

Communication Principles

Several factors influence communication. The communication process can break down. Decoding or interpretations can vary. Feedback may not be provided. When so much can go wrong, what can we do to ensure that communication is effective?

The responsibility of communication is heavier on the sender than the receiver. For this reason, it is essential for the sender to be precise. A well-thought-out message or communication will incorporate several elements such as the choice of words, nonverbal cues, and an understanding of the audience for whom the message is intended, among others. The underlying principle is that the message should be received in the way the sender intended. Any ambiguity would result in an incorrect or undesirable response from the recipient.

It also helps if communication does not contradict or conflict with behavior. A messy parent lecturing a child on the importance of cleanliness, for example. Punctuality being preached by a senior with a record for tardiness would not elicit the correct response from subordinates either. People's attention is drawn to behaviors and nonverbal cues as much as to the message itself. Ensure consistency and the communication will be more effective, and as a result, the outcome will be more desirable.

Flexibility is another vital principle when communicating— for example, assessing an audience and deciding whether or not to be formal or informal. An insightful, well-crafted speech or presentation could lose impact if the speaker failed to connect with the audience personally.

What would be the impact of a response to an urgent message if the recipient were to reply much later and after the urgency was handled? How effective would your discipline efforts be if you were to communicate hours, days, or even weeks after the incident occurred? Timeliness is an underemphasized principle of communication. Every communication demands a response within a specific timeframe for it to be effective.

While much of the onus of communication falls on the sender, the recipient carries some responsibility. Feedback, for instance, is crucial to making communication effective. If a message or communication comes as a shock or surprise, the recipient should seek clarification.

The complexity involved in communication is also why employers consider communication skills as a criterion when recruiting. Learning and developing good communication skills are vital for success in your personal life and career. It can help build your network, be it personal, social, or professional. For some, communication comes naturally, while for others, it takes time and practice. Either way, both communication and interpersonal skills can be enhanced.

Chapter 1: Effective Communication

What is Effective Communication?

Communication, as we have previously explored, is the process of sending messages through a medium. But communication doesn't end there. The message needs to be decoded as well. The process ends when the recipient receives the message as the sender intended. We're also agreed on why humans communicate. As higher thinking beings, humans endeavor to make sense of the world, and we communicate as we need to share that sense with others. We've also learned that communication is established through verbal and nonverbal messages.

Since we know so much, how can we still flounder when it comes to communication?

Let's consider an example.

> "I want you to clean your room," says a mother to her ten-year-old. Trying to please the mother, the child jumps off her bed and begins to pick up the clothes scattered on the floor. Satisfied that her communication elicited the desired response, the

mother leaves. When she returns twenty minutes later, the mother is sorely disappointed.

"I thought I asked you to clean up," she exclaims, frustrated.

"But I did," insists the child.

"I don't see it," states the mother. "Your study table is disorganized, your shoes are not in their place, and there's dust everywhere," she huffs. "So, what did you do?" she questions.

"I made my bed and put my clothes and toys away."

Let's consider another scenario.

A customer walks into a coffee house and says "I'd like a large, triple-shot, sugar-free, low-fat latte, please."

It's evident that the customer ordering coffee is more skilled at communication than the mother. What would we think if the mother and the coffee customer were the same person? Why is it that we can order our coffee with such precision but mess up other communication forms?

Did these examples give you a reason to pause and reflect on your communication effectiveness? Are you now wondering what you could have said or how you could have pitched your candidacy for that raise or promotion and then received it? Perhaps you're now contemplating what it was about your dinner invitation refusal that left your mother in tears? Can communication play such a crucial role in a person's successes and failures?

It seems that regardless of the situation—at home, in a social context, or at the workplace—one thing will make or break the experience. Communication—a skill we began to acquire before we were born and one that, over time, comes to us as naturally as brushing our teeth, crossing the road, or tying our shoelaces. We do it each day without a second thought. As we navigate life, we come to understand that communication in everyday experiences is an essential process, and a skill that will help us make sense of things. We go through the process and never consider whether we're effective communicators or not.

Clearly, communication goes above the simplified definition of "information exchange." What more could it entail? Is it the emotion and intention behind the information? Could improving listening skills help us ascertain the full meaning of what's being said? Will it allow the sender to feel heard and understood? Will our body language and approachability make the other person feel less hesitant and more valued?

More often than not, when we try to communicate, something goes awry. We say something, but the other person hears something else, and misunderstandings, frustration, and conflicts result.

Just like the mother was frustrated that the daughter missed several elements of her room that required cleaning, the customer from the earlier example would not have been pleased with her coffee had the barista handed her an ordinary latte. For communication to be successful, one of its key characteristics is completeness and clarity. The mother's message needed to be clear and complete, just like the coffee customer had been with the barista. A list, for instance, would have allowed the child to make better decisions and avoided all the fuss and miscommunication later.

Communication is never simple. It's a complicated process with a number of elements that attribute to its failure or success. One of these is the principle of feedback. An older child would have perhaps thought to seek feedback and clarity at the outset and subsequently would have fared better.

Could the mother have avoided miscommunication had she drawn the child's attention to all the elements she considered ideal when she asked for the room to be cleaned?

For many of us, learning these skills can deepen our connections to others, build greater trust and respect, and improve teamwork, problem-solving, and overall social and emotional health.

Principles of Effective Communication

What can we do for our communication to be more effective? Let's outline some of the principles of effective communication.

Communication is necessary, whether it is interpersonal or general. To be an effective communicator, you need to keep the following in mind:

During Interpersonal Communication

- Treat people with respect.
- Avoid interrupting others.
- Make ethical choices. You never know who is listening and being inspired by what you say.
- Do not say what you do not mean.
- Respect the other person's opinion.
- Challenge perceptions not people.
- Accept that everyone makes mistakes.
- Respect confidentiality.

During General Communication

- Have a goal or purpose to the conversation.
- Don't just hear. Listen!
- Be clear. Do not make ambiguous statements.

- Be persuasive but be willing to consider another's point of view.
- Stay organized with your thoughts.
- Use stories to get your point across.
- Be consistent in your views and opinions. Don't keep contradicting yourself. It will reflect poorly on you.
- Give adequate information. Too much or too little information can create unnecessary problems. Be succinct.
- Always understand your audience and tailor your message accordingly.

Verbal and Nonverbal Communication

Nonverbal Communication

Even before we could string together words, we communicated through gestures, sounds, and facial expressions. Is it therefore so surprising that we say a lot more through our body than we do through our words?

If we sit leaned back, we appear at ease. However, if we lean forward, we're eager and interested. If we stand with our hands by our side, we're comfortable. But if we cross our arms across our chest, we come off as defensive. We communicate with our bodies. While we spend a lot of time and effort being polite or diplomatic with our word choices, we don't consider what our body language is saying.

Consider this: Verbal communication uses one channel as it is picked up by the recipient's auditory processing sense—their ears. However, nonverbal communication can be transmitted and deciphered by all five senses. Is it then prudent to simply make just the verbal form of communication more effective?

Why else should we consider honing our nonverbal communication skills?

Simple.

Language or verbal communication is cultural-based and an acquired skill. It is not a common denominator across the world. You wouldn't call a Scot a jock, nor an American a yank, nor an Indian a coolie, and so on. Cross-cultural misunderstandings arise because words/terms such as these don't quite mean the same everywhere. It could be quite innocent in one part of the world and a slur in another.

Nonverbal communication, however, is instinctive. It is not taught, but it is learned. And it is the same the world over. No matter where you were born or what your native language is, if you accidentally stub your toe, you are not going to scream "yes" and jump up and down with joy.

People tend to trust nonverbal communication because (a) it is universal, and (b) it is harder to fake.

Types of Nonverbal Communication

The common types of nonverbal communication include:

Facial Communication - Humans are extremely expressive. We can convey myriads of emotions without saying a single word. Secondly, facial expressions are universal. This means there are fewer chances of them being misinterpreted. The expressions of anger, confusion, desire, disgust, fear, joy, sorrow, and surprise are the same across cultures and languages.

Postures or Body Movement - The way a person moves or carries themselves reveals a lot about them to the world. We can get a fair idea of a person by the way he or she sits, walks, stands, or even holds their head. People who sit straight or stand tall with their heads held high are perceived to be more confident than others.

Gestures - Gestures are an integral part of our daily life and the most direct body language signals. However, they are not universal and may have different connotations. For example, raising the index and middle fingers to represent a V means victory or peace in most countries. But, in countries like the UK and Australia, it is considered offensive. The OK sign carries a positive message in most

English-speaking countries. However, in countries like Russia and Germany, it is considered offensive.

Touch - Touch is another integral part of nonverbal communication that says a great deal. From a warm bear hug to a cursory shake of the hands, or even a pat on the back, they all convey a lot to someone perceptive enough.

Distance - Heard of the term proxemics? Coined by anthropologist Edward T. Hall, it refers to the proximity or the distance between people while interacting. While everyone needs personal space, the need differs depending on the situation or the relationship between the people interacting. The closer the relationship, the closer the distance and vice versa.

Since nonverbal communication can impact our messages to a great extent, consistency in signals play a crucial role in how our messages are interpreted. Let's examine some of these briefly.

Nonverbal Signals

How we sit, stand, walk, what our hands are doing, where we are looking—all of these and more affect how others perceive and interpret our communication. Often referred to as kinesics, our body language provides the recipient with clues that will help them to determine the speaker's attitude and feelings toward a particular communication. For instance, head-nodding shows engagement and listening. It reassures the speaker that they are being heard and it encourages them to continue. Fidgeting with a pencil or clicking on a pen would convey boredom and excessive energy. These signals are most often observed during long meetings or conferences.

Haptics, or communication by touch, is a nonverbal signal that carries a tremendous risk of being misinterpreted. A hug at home could convey affection or reassurance. The same innocent hug at the workplace would be highly inappropriate, whereas the comfort that same hug can offer someone who is grieving could surpass that of any heartfelt words.

Proxemics or distance is another nonverbal signal that affects communication. Everyone craves personal space and sets rules on what is considered an infringement of their personal space. Of course, we make exceptions for people we hold dear. Friends, family, loved ones can all step into our personal space without making us uncomfortable. If a person grew up in a semi-urban or rural setting, they would be uncomfortable with the lack of personal space typical of cosmopolitan or metropolitan cities.

It isn't enough to just be mindful of the signals we send out. When interacting with others, we must also be quick to identify what the other person is feeling. Learning to pick up on these clues and their "intensity" can help us to mitigate certain situations. For instance, if a person frowns while reading instructions, it might indicate that they could use some help. In sales or customer service, identifying a nonverbal expression such as a frown can help you provide assistance before it is asked for. This will invariably lead to a positive interaction.

Paraverbal Signals (Spoken)

The second set of signals that we give out are called paraverbal signals. These signals can be divided into two categories—spoken and written. The spoken paraverbal signals are also called vocalics. These include the pitch, frequency, and volume of our tone. It would also cover verbal fillers and quality.

Vocalics are also a set of signals that aren't taught to us. We learn these instinctively as we navigate through life. A toddler, for instance, hasn't attended English grammar classes, and yet he or she is capable of recognizing that a high-pitch at the end of a sentence indicates that the sentence is a question. Similarly, a sarcastic "well done" said to a child who might have spilled their juice is counterproductive. The child will probably grin and assume you don't mind spills and messes and continue to do both. Since that was not the desired outcome, it is evident that the message was misinterpreted as it wasn't paired with the appropriate paraverbal signals.

Consider another example. If you are soft-spoken, you are considered meek. A meek person can't establish authority unless they alter their delivery technique. Shouting on the other hand conveys anger. Simply raising one's pitch will therefore not have the desired effect (establishing authority).

For any communication to be effective your message must match your signals. A presenter rushing through a speech or presentation could be seen as lacking in confidence or anxious. This would directly affect his or her credibility.

To align these two (signals and messages) you must be clear about what attitude and emotion need to follow your message.

Consider this scenario.

> You find mistakes in the task you assigned to a subordinate at work. You summon the subordinate to your office, shout, point fingers, and perhaps even pace behind your desk.
>
> Before you launch into a tirade take a moment to understand what result you desire.
>
> - Do you want to communicate your frustration and disappointment? Yes, that was achieved with a loud pitch.
>
> - Do you want the subordinate to cower and shake? Yes, that was achieved with an aggressive attitude.

If, however, you wanted to project approachability and an attitude more suitable to a mentor, by allowing your emotions to take control and not considering your nonverbal and paraverbal signals, you achieved the opposite. Calmly explaining the error and giving further (clearer) instructions would have helped the subordinate to rectify the situation.

Paraverbal Signals (Written)

As with its spoken counterpart, paraverbal signals in writing play a crucial role in conveying our emotions and our attitude. These are clues the reader will leverage to decipher the intention and meaning of our communication. As with all other nonverbal communication forms, certain rules and guidelines need to be followed to avoid miscommunication. Using capital letters in written communication is similar to shouting. How would a colleague then respond to a request for help with a task or project if the message were written in capitals and punctuated with exclamation points? Authority and credibility are also communicated through written nonverbal communication. What image are you projecting if your written communication breaks all rules of grammar?

Perceptive people go beyond gestures and words. They are quick to identify the all-encompassing meaning of a communication by detecting nonverbal communication. Our nonverbal communication is equally and sometimes more important than our verbal communication because it carries the emotion and attitude that reinforces or undermines our message.

Verbal Communication

Verbal messages are communicated through language. Language developed with the "need" to communicate on a more comprehensive and complex level. If you think about it, it's impossible to share anything beyond emotions and feelings with gestures. Imagine trying to explain theology, nuclear science, or something less complex, like crop rotation, through gestures!

Language doesn't come to us as instinctively as nonverbal communication. It must be learned. At its root, language is nothing more than symbols and meanings attached to those symbols. Since language differs from place to place, region to region, and country to country, it is intertwined with culture. It forms the basis of our identities.

Ironically enough, it is this symbolic nature of verbal communication that, when used in an abstract manner, can cause misunderstandings. It is also a reason we pair it, consciously and otherwise, with nonverbal signals to give it context. The effectiveness of our verbal communications is increased by the social norms we learn as we grow. How many times have you been baffled when actions come before words?

Consider the following:

- Someone swings your car door open and sits in your passenger seat before asking whether they can hitch a ride with you.

- Someone leaves in the middle of a meeting or presentation only to return and then ask to be excused because they needed to use the bathroom.

How would you react to these or similar situations? Would you not consider the person to be impolite? Implicit rules, roles, and routines teach us acceptable and unacceptable forms of verbal communication. And we rely heavily on these to guide us through our verbal communications as we grow. We also come to realize that communication rules change based on our environment. The way we speak at home, with our friends, at a university, and at work, will all differ widely.

For a communication to be effective, we must accurately interpret verbal messages as this interpretation is co-created. Communication is not a pipeline. A message doesn't simply go from the sender to the receiver as is. Multiple influencers, or noise, add layers and meanings to the communication. These invariably lead to varied interpretations of the original message, often leading to undesired responses or behaviors.

Our interaction frequency with people helps us cut out the "noise" and keep interpretations true. A new person at work might find a gruff boss intimidating. However, for someone who has been there a while, they would probably understand that "gruffness" is a natural state for the boss, and hence, be less or not at all intimidated by it.

Whether in a social or professional context, we must make effective use of our communication skills and improve our ability to cut out the noise and interpret messages.

Creating Persuasive and Memorable Messages

We communicate for three reasons—to convey our ideas, collect information from people, and change relationships.

Let's first explore how we convey ideas. So, when we try to communicate, a part of the challenge we face is converting our thoughts into messages that are (a) clear and (b) impactful. How can we do that? By grabbing attention. What is the best way to catch somebody's attention? Through persuasive and memorable communication.

While all ideas have merit, some are invariably rejected as they lack the speaker's persuasive ability. Consider the brands you love and why you love them. Why did you pick that jar of honey from the shelf even though it isn't your go-to brand? What caught your eye about its tag line or packaging? Think about the advertisement that made you laugh, poke the person next to you and say, "Did you see that? I love that!" Or the one that made you frown, shake your head in disapproval, and at the next party, you bring it up with "Did you see the gall of that company? And their product campaign?"

Persuasive and memorable messages aren't limited to advertisements and marketing or political campaigns. Think of the loan officer at the bank that sees thousands of applications in a year. The loan (idea) is accompanied by the need (a persuasive pitch). And it's the loan officer's job to decide which was compelling enough for him to grant.

So, for ideas to be persuasive, they need to grab attention. There are several ways to grab someone's attention. You can surprise them, offer them a puzzle, or you can offer them a story. Think of whodunit movies. Thrillers, murder mysteries, suspense, horrors, and such. These genres offer the viewer a puzzle to solve. Now consider movies or books like Anne Frank. Why did it catch the world's attention? Emotions. The story tugged at our heartstrings and left a strong impression.

Credibility is another thing an idea needs. Lies and deceit are intertwined with survival. Think camouflage. Chameleons. Humans are no different. Lying and deception is an art that we've mastered. The ability to cut through layers and identify deceit is a skill that most humans have acquired. For an idea to be persuasive, it needs to be credible. It needs to pass the human lie detector test.

Being truthful and real can make or break anything. You wouldn't call your boss and ask to be excused claiming you're sick while you're at a party with loud background music, would you? Consider fairytales. Children believe them because they trust their parents (authoritative figures) who tell them such stories.

As we navigate through life, these lessons stay with us. They become our deciding parameters. How many of us would trust a lesser-known brand or a new entrant in the market? We come to trust brands, authoritative figures, etc. We tend to stick to them because we know they are credible.

The final essential facet of creating memorable messages is to keep them simple. List a key idea first, give the details later, but keep linking back to the key idea so it's not forgotten. This is perhaps why a photograph with a news article works so well. Why videos and social media like Snapchat and Twitter are incredibly popular. You say less with more (the old adage is a picture is worth a thousand words). You share a vivid story. The more vivid the story, the more memorable it becomes. And the more popular you become. And your popularity establishes the effectiveness of your communication.

Asking Thoughtful Questions

Aside from conveying our ideas, another reason that prompts communication is the need to collect information. We do this by asking questions. Consider the interview process. The interviewer needs to gather the information to decide whether the candidate sitting across from him is suitable for the position.

Questions are also prompted when we require help with something. Figuring your way around a new neighborhood would require you to stop and ask for directions. Finding the correct item on your grocery list when in a new or less familiar store will prompt you to question the store employee for the correct aisle number and directions. We can wander aimlessly in the retail stores till we find what we want. Or we could simply just ask for help.

> Consider this scenario. You need cherries. You ask the store employee where you might find them. The employee gives you the aisle number and location. However, when you arrive at the spot, to your dismay, you can't find the cherries you wanted. There's a different aisle for frozen cherries, all the way across the store is another aisle for candied cherries, and somewhere along the way is the aisle for the fresh cherries you wanted. You're frustrated, the store employee feels useless, and the entire experience becomes a negative one.

- How could you have avoided this outcome? By asking thoughtful questions. *Where can I find the fresh cherries?*

- How could the store employee have avoided this outcome? By asking thoughtful questions. *What kind of cherries did you want? Fresh, frozen, or candied?*

Let's go back to marketing for a moment. Products and services are designed around a *gap* or a *need* or a *want* for a *service*. What's the best way to show people they "need" a product or service?

By agitating them.

> *Are you afraid of...? Then you need this product.*
>
> *Can't wake up in the morning—you should try this beverage.*
>
> *Don't want to invest in the market? How about a safer alternative with guaranteed returns?*

And where did all this information come from? Questions in surveys, of course.

The more direct your question, the better.

Consider these examples.

> **Person A:** Where would you like to go for dinner?
>
> **Person B:** I don't know. Wherever you'd like to go.

The above is a perfect example of an open-ended question that we've probably asked dozens of times, to which we've received a vague, undecided response that's probably left us sighing with frustration and defeat. What could we have done differently?

> **Person A:** Would you like Indian or Italian for dinner?
>
> **Person B:** I feel like some antipasto!

Here's another:

> **Person A:** Did you have your medication after breakfast?
>
> **Person B:** Er…I think so.
>
> **Person A:** Did you have your medication, including the new one the doctor prescribed yesterday?
>
> **Person B:** No, I missed that one. Thanks for reminding me.

Effective communication isn't just about conveying our ideas in a way that preserves the integrity of the message. It is also about eliciting the correct response, learning to ask the right questions, and getting the feedback and information we require to make better decisions and correct choices.

Perceptions Versus Reality

If you speak like that, people will think you're rude.

If you dress like this, people will think you're a slob.

If you don't wake up early, people will think you're lazy. It doesn't matter that you worked the whole night.

How many times have we heard such feedback from others? Perceptions or impressions play a crucial role in our lives. Chances are, you've been the recipient and the designer of such perceptions.

Every day, we perceive people and objects around us. We leverage our experiences to help us make sense of people and things. When we encounter something new, our experiences help us to filter and organize information. Take, for instance, a new person at the office.

> You know nothing about them. What would you think about them if they had a tattoo or piercings? What would you feel about them if they dressed too formally or too informally? Your experiences help you make decisions about that person. If your best friend has a tattoo, you'll probably warm up to the

new person faster. However, if you've had terrible experiences with people who express themselves with ink, you're more likely to stay far away from the new person.

Sometimes the information we get is contradictory, and it changes the way we think. The politician with the perfect personal life and political career demands your respect until the opposition digs up dirt. Then you question what you know and how you think and feel about the politician.

The way we communicate and behave with people is directly affected by our perception of them as well. If we favor an object or person, we respond differently to them.

Consider this scenario.

> A supervisor has assigned you a task. After you've submitted the assignment, the supervisor identifies several mistakes. Your reaction to the feedback and criticism that follows will differ based on whether you have a rapport with your supervisor. For instance, if you like and respect your supervisor, you'll consider the feedback, recheck your work, and feel like you've grown and learned something new.
>
> However, if you neither like nor respect your supervisor, you'll feel bitter. You'll lament on how the supervisor is making things difficult for you. And

at some point, you'll even question whether or not the supervisor is qualified to make such decisions based on perceptions you've formed of the supervisor.

Facts about Perceptions:

- First and last impressions are powerful forces.

- We tend to put more importance on initial impressions than later impressions.

- Physical and environmental cues like clothing, grooming, attractiveness, and material objects, influence people's impressions.

Our self-concept is also formed through our interactions with others and their reactions to us. For instance, you'll consider yourself to be polite, well-mannered, and funny, if enough people have shared that feedback with you.

Our sense of self-concept also develops through comparisons. For instance, you'll judge yourself to be more intelligent than your sibling or less athletic than your spouse. Comparisons and forming self-concepts isn't a bad thing. Not until our reference group becomes inappropriate. Measuring your athletic ability with that of your favorite athlete would be unreasonable and have negative consequences.

When communicating with people we're relatively unfamiliar with, it helps to alter perceptions if we choose to believe that their intentions are honest. By assuming that there's malice in uncertainty surrounding the circumstances, we become more skeptical and jaded. This affects the effectiveness of our communication with people in general. Here's a quick look at how checking perception with reality will positively change our behavior toward people.

1. Open-mindedness

When we condition ourselves not to find malice or ill-intent, it allows us to be curious about people's actions and communications. We become less judgmental and slower to assume that the person meant to hurt us. This affects our communication with people as we're more inclined toward learning the "how" and "why" of things.

2. Empathy

When we learn about other people's situations that govern specific actions and communications, it broadens our thought process and allows us to consider the other person's circumstances. We can thus connect with people at a deeper level. It also helps us to see the context behind their actions.

3. **Willingness to Help Others**

When our mind is less focused on anger, we assess situations with a broader lens. By connecting with the other person, we find it easier to lend a helping hand. Bringing positivity in a social or professional environment has a ripple effect. When we react to a negative situation with understanding and empathy, it equips others to do the same as well.

Perception checking is a good way to monitor our reactions to people and objects. It will also help check our perceptions of communication. We can use several internal and external strategies to control our perceptions. One of the easiest ways is to question the basis of your perception. Another approach could be to use other people to verify our perceptions.

When our perception forming process improves, the effect spills into elements that increase the effectiveness of our communication—listening skills, for instance.

Effectiveness in Other Forms of Communication

Criticism and Constructive Feedback

Feedback and criticism are a part of our daily lives. We've all been givers, receivers, or both. You could be speaking with your housekeeper about how certain expectations were not met or performing an annual review, or giving feedback on ideas and presentations. Your supervisor at work could be outlining all the ways in which performance expectations were not met, or how tasks didn't meet briefs. Either way, a lot can go wrong when criticism or feedback is not presented in a constructive and actionable manner.

Criticism is an important channel for growth as it allows people to identify areas of improvement. Development and improvement are essential as, without either, we'd stagnate.

There are a few strategies that, when adopted, can deliver criticism effectively and constructively.

How to Provide Constructive Criticism

Use the Sandwich Approach

Let's revisit our mother and child example from earlier.

"I want you to clean your room," says a mother to her ten-year-old. Trying to please the mother, the child jumps off her bed and begins to pick up the clothes scattered on the floor. Satisfied that her communication elicited the desired response, the mother leaves. When she returns twenty minutes later, the mother is sorely disappointed.

"I thought I asked you to clean up," she exclaims, frustrated.

"But I did," insists the child.

"I don't see it," states the mother. "Your study table is disorganized, your shoes are not in their place, and there's dust everywhere," she huffs.

Imagine the child's predicament in this situation. The mother's initial communication was vague, and her feedback is harsh and includes several undesirable nonverbal clues. What probably made matters worse is that the mother didn't recognize what the child had done correctly.

Consider the following feedback.

"I see you've made your bed and put your clothes away. Your room does look neater. Thank you. But you've missed your study table. Could you take a minute to arrange your books and your stationery as well? I also like how you've arranged your toys. Perhaps you could do the same with your shoes? If you're unsure of how to do that, I could help."

By "sandwiching" the criticism or feedback between specific praise statements and offering assistance, the child would not feel as devastated as before. It would preserve her enthusiasm for the next task, grow (not strip away) her self-confidence, and encourage growth in a positive and supportive environment.

"I" instead of "You" Approach

One of the reasons people dread giving and receiving criticism is that it puts people on the defensive. This happens when a person feels targeted or criticized. One of the principles of effective interpersonal communication was to target behaviors, not people. How can we provide feedback in a way that doesn't make the person feel like the criticism is about them?

Use "I" phrases instead of "You."

Consider the following scenarios.

"You shouldn't go out dressed like that."

A statement like that would instantly put the receiver on the defensive.

"I envy your bold color choices. However, I feel like the baby pink would be more suitably matched with a white or blue rather than that shade of green. Should we check your wardrobe for something comfortable and festive in a pastel tone?"

By using "I feel" statements and offering help, the receiver would be less likely to see the criticism as aggressive and would not go on the defensive. Instead, you'd arouse their curiosity to explore an alternate way of doing something. Here, the feedback would be seen as advice, not judgment.

Conflict and Resolution

Conflict is an inevitable part of life. We've all been in situations where we've been in disagreement with other people and where our goals and needs have clashed with those of others. Often, such situations are easily resolved. However, there have been situations where conflict results in intense personal animosity.

Whether in a social or professional context, conflicts can bring to the surface hidden problems which when resolved can benefit us significantly.

Unexpected benefits of conflicts and their resolution:

- The process of resolving conflict nurtures greater understanding among people. It expands awareness and provides insight into how people can achieve their goals without subverting others.

- In a group or team situation, conflict resolution can further group cohesion. It helps build stronger mutual respect. It also reinforces people's ability to work together.

- Difficult situations like conflicts can boost self-knowledge. It pushes people to examine their goals and expectations, helps them to identify what is important, sharpens focus, and enhances effectiveness.

Equally, conflict can be damaging. If it isn't handled effectively, conflict can turn into personal dislike, breakdown teamwork, and lead to disengagement. In a professional context, it can be the cause for high attrition. Conflicts lead to lower productivity and its frequency can create a negative work environment.

Conflict Resolution

The process involving conflict resolution typically involves some or all of the following:

- To begin with, both sides must acknowledge that a problem exists.

- They must be ready to address the issue—instead of simply voicing differences and assigning blame, both sides must be willing to understand the other's concerns as well.

- The focus should be on changing behaviors and approaches, rather than targeting people and leading to greater negative feelings.

- Both sides must work together, patiently, to identify triggers, agree on a plan to address differences and if the situation requires it, reach a compromise.

Communicating Effectively with Technology

Our lives are so enmeshed with technology that it's difficult to imagine how we'd survive without it. Think of all the times you checked the weather app before stepping out. The chats with friends, family, and even colleagues before you're dressed for work. Emails sent from the phone while you're commuting via bus or train. Many aspects of our day-to-day work, and even chores, can be completed or monitored with just a few keystrokes.

While technology has enabled faster communication, it has also opened doors to miscommunications. Changing language, for instance. How many of us text with complete sentences? All the abbreviations, the chat lingos, and emoji usage that have become part of our everyday vocabulary. Think of all the platforms that have become accessible to us—Twitter, Snapchat, Instagram, Facebook, TikTok, Messengers, and whatnot. Anyone who has anything to say can easily find one or multiple such platforms and communicate their ideas and opinions. However, just because we have so many avenues for communication and we're happy to use them doesn't mean we're effective communicators.

One challenge we face in the digital age is modifying our communication mediums to retain effectiveness. For instance, the nonverbal cues we rely on—facial expressions, hand gestures, pitch, and tone—they've all been replaced with white screens and hastily typed messages. How are we then to infer what we would have normally inferred? Misinterpretations become rife, and conflicts ensue.

Think of how many times you thought you were venting about a client to a colleague but sent the message to the client instead. An internal email that got cc'd and bcc'd several times and ended up being shared with external clients or vendors. A personal message to a spouse that went to the boss. Something you typed that autocorrect decided sounded better a different way and ended up embarrassing you. Confusion and setbacks at work because messages were too short and vague—all this and more has become our reality and a communication barrier.

So how do we ensure that technology-based communication works more to our advantage than disadvantage?

Get Visual but Selectively

One of the things about digital communication that opens doors to miscommunication is the lack of nonverbal cues like tone and facial expressions. Could that "good job" be praise or sarcasm? How can you tell? Worse still is when you receive a "gd jb." Is that indicative of the sender being pressed for time, or is the sender perfunctory or dismissive? How do you know? The same message accompanied with a smiley face or a dancing person or fireworks would put you at ease, no?

While emojis, stickers, and GIF's can substitute for some nonverbal cues, many of the older generation, or if you'd prefer the pre-smartphone generation, find them awkward and sometimes even downright distasteful. In a personal conversation, sure, use whatever tickles you. In professional communication, however, be more discerning about what you send. The simpler, the better.

Be Prompt but Considerate

Think of the new friend you made further east than you've ever traveled or even one several states over and in a different time zone. You message them. They message back. No one worries about time differences. After all, it's never too early nor too late to share a meme that will make the other person snicker. But what if you did that to your boss or an important client? Would they be as appreciative of several incoming message dings at 2 a.m.? Send your assignments, upload your files, reply to those pending emails—but do so after you've checked the clock. If you're working late, schedule the email to be sent automatically at a more reasonable hour, for instance.

Length and Punctuation

We've moved from glaring at typewriters and keyboards clicking one key at a time, to using only "thumbs" to type messages on our smartphones, to now just sliding one finger across a virtual keyboard and software automatically drafting our messages for us. We're quick to send and often say "oops, fat fingers" when we get something wrong. Again, the principle of selectivity applies to our messages. Send a "hru" to your best friend, but not your client. Opt for length when you need to convey genuine emotions. "Sorry" doesn't stand a chance when you can take an extra minute to draft a more sincere apology.

Permanence

Today, what we say is no longer heard by a limited audience, nor is it forgotten with time. Everything we communicate through technology is recorded somewhere. And what complicates matters is that we see ourselves as anonymous when we are online, but the truth is we are not. That response to a post on Facebook or comment at the end of someone's blog will link back to us, and it's all retrievable with a few keystrokes. It's available to future employers as well. Permanence has a new meaning (not just memory retention) and carries consequences like never before. What we say becomes part of our identity, and it must be said after careful consideration.

Choose your Medium

Most people are uncomfortable with change. We get familiar with one form of communication and default to it every time. Constantly sending messages through one preferred chat messenger, for instance, isn't always conducive to efficient communication. Consider your medium before you communicate. Think of the appropriateness of the medium and whether it will simplify or add complexity to the situation. Since technology-based communication can be emotionless, an apology or conflict resolution might be better handled in person than an email.

Benefit of the Doubt

While technology-based communication can be emotionless to a large extent, surprisingly enough, it can trigger powerful emotions in the receiver. This happens when the communication is vague and open for interpretation. In previous sections of this chapter, we've explored how we use our experiences to interpret nonverbal cues (perception versus reality), or how we're prone to attaching meaning to communication that lacks such cues. This is true of digital communication, as well. Consider how your message or email might be interpreted and modify it before you send it. And if you've received a communication that invoked powerful emotions, instead of sending a hasty and rude response that underscores your disapproval, take some time to settle down and review the communication from a clearer lens.

Chapter 2 Part 1: Constructive Communication

What is Constructive Communication?

As a quick recap, we've discussed that communication implies conveying one's ideas and thoughts to others. We've also explored what effective communication is—the recipient receiving the message as the sender intended—and how to make our communication more efficient.

Constructive communication occurs when both parties—the sender and the recipient—endeavor to listen to each other, build new ideas, find common ground, and understand.

Let's consider a typical playground scene where two girls are sitting side-by-side on swings and talking.

>**Child A:** My mom gave me a new doll for Christmas.

>**Child B:** I watched Frozen 2 on TV last evening.

>**Child A:** She has the prettiest blue eyes, and they close when you lay her down.

Child B: I felt sad when Elsa almost died in the movie.

In this instance, the two girls are engaged in what seems like a conversation with each other, but it isn't. They're both speaking, but neither is listening to the other. It's more like two monologues happening in parallel. This is not what constructive communication looks like.

A constructive communication happens when both parties listen to each other closely, accept different opinions, understand each other's viewpoints and interests, and find common ground that helps them define further actions. For communication to be constructive, both people need to feel involved in the process.

Communication needs to be monitored on three levels for it to be constructive.

Subject Level: In the previous example, one girl spoke about her Christmas present while the other talked about a movie. This is the subject level of their conversation. For their discussion to have been constructive, the two girls should have been communicating about the same subject or topic. Deviating from the topic causes issues and miscommunications, and hence, the communication cannot be labeled as constructive. To avoid such a scenario, both parties, in this case the two girls, should have determined a subject or goal before beginning their discussion.

Relationship Level: When we communicate with someone we're not too fond of, we're less likely to be open, honest, and 'giving' in the conversation. Think back to the 'perception versus reality' discussion. The way we communicate and behave with people is directly linked to our perception of them. When we're engaged in a conversation with someone we don't like or respect, what is the likelihood of us being agreeable to their perspective? Would we make the same effort to find common ground or accept different views? We should monitor communication at the relationship level as well for it to be constructive, even with a less-liked person.

Emotional Level: Emotions are part of life; we cannot avoid them, and certainly not in a conversation. Two friends engaged in a discussion about the recent election, for example, will share their views on which candidate is better suited to lead. The emotions triggered during this conversation will depend on whether both friends prefer the same candidate or not. If they prefer different candidates, the discussion will soon turn heated, and the subsequent rise of emotions will disturb the communication flow on the subject level. What's worse is that these same emotions will also negatively influence their relationship level. So, monitoring emotional levels during a conversation is a vital aspect of keeping communication constructive.

What is Deconstructive Communication?

People often verbalize their feelings during communication. And this is expected. How else will you foster understanding and resolve disputes if you don't? The aim of such a conversation or communication is to be constructive—to find a solution or determine future action. But what happens when our goal changes? What kind of communication takes place when we're certain we're right, and we're not inclined to listen to the other person? Worse, what happens when we aim to persecute the other person?

Think of all the 'I-told-you-so' conversations that you've either been at the giving or receiving end of. Did you feel at 'peace' and 'empathized with' when someone said it to you? And what was your attitude or intention when you said it to someone else? It probably wasn't to help them find a solution.

These form the crux of deconstructive communication, where instead of fostering peace and understanding, we introduce greater conflict and dissolution.

Common Destructive Communication Habits

Most people have never heard of the different communication types and are even less familiar with negative and positive communication forms. Why? Because communication is something we learn by watching and listening to the people around us.

If someone you grew up with had a penchant for leaning out the window and launching into a foul tirade at a fellow driver for what may or may not have been their mistake, chances are you probably do the same. If someone close to you during your childhood often motivated you with sentences that began with "If you don't...then I will..." chances are you probably use the same motivational style in your adulthood.

Since communication is mirrored, most people are either subconsciously constructive or deconstructive. They don't quite know what they're doing wrong, or even *if* they're doing something wrong.

But what if we could wean out the negatives? Remember all the confrontational or distasteful conversations you were part of or the ones you avoided. What if communication could be free of all that?

Let's examine some habits that are barriers to constructive communication.

Interrupting

To stop someone else mid-way during a conversation is a common habit. We're often told it's impolite or rude to do so. How many of us take that seriously? How many of us contribute interruption to destructive communication?

Why is Interrupting a Barrier to Communication?

Think back to some of your "oops" moments. What were some of the presumptions that prompted you to interrupt? How differently would the conversation have been had you let the speaker finish?

"Get to the point quickly, please. I have a meeting I must rush to."

"I already know what you're going to say, and the answer is no."

"Before you continue, I would like to add…"

When we interrupt, several things happen:

On a Subject Level: When the speaker is stopped mid-way, you don't hear everything they were going to say. You don't get the full picture—that unfinished sentence or thought might have been useful. It might have included an aspect that you did not expect to hear.

On a Relationship Level: Interrupting someone changes the dynamics of communication. From a conversation where both partners are equal, it becomes an exchange where one partner dominates while the other becomes submissive.

On an Emotional Level: You might offend or upset the person you interrupted. It invokes feelings of resentment, bitterness, and even anger. They are then unwilling to continue the conversation, and even if they do, they aren't as open as they would have been. Relationship levels worsen, and this has far-reaching consequences if the conversation were an attempt at conflict resolution.

Conjecture

In situations when we do not listen until the end, we do not hear the other person's complete argument or point, and we fail to understand what the other person was going to say. Since there are information gaps, we fill them by conjecturing. We become presumptuous. As a result, misunderstandings occur, and negative emotions surface.

Let's consider an example. Ellie's parents are separated. Tom is Ellie's father. He loves her and often takes her for various outings. Recently he has become less available. Sarah, Ellie's mother, notices this and "concludes" that Tom isn't spending as much time with Ellie because she is naughty. She says to Ellie, "Your father does not want to see you because you do not behave..." Ellie is upset and too young to understand what went wrong or what aspects of her behavior upset her father. She feels offended and unloved by both her parents. How could this have been avoided? If Sarah had called Tom and asked him about his reduced presence, she might have learned that he was devoting more time to a project as he wanted to save up for Ellie's birthday.

Ambiguity in Information Perception

Information perception and ambiguity go hand-in-hand. They also present barriers to constructive communication. We discussed earlier how humans have the tendency to 'attach' meaning to verbal and nonverbal cues. As such, different people can interpret the same communication differently, and all of these interpretations can quite easily be dramatically opposed to what the sender intended. Paying attention, listening better, asking questions, and providing feedback are some of the ways we can prevent ourselves from making quick conclusions and distorting the actual meaning of a communication.

Clarifying Questions

The solution to the issues of conjecture and ambiguity in information perception is to be active listeners. A key aspect that separates active listeners from passive listeners is the ability to process information and ask questions.

On a Subject Level: When we miss certain points during a discussion, either because we were preoccupied or distracted, we don't quite grasp the discussion on a subject level. By asking for clarification, we open ourselves to the opportunity to understand the communication as the speaker intended it.

On a Relationship Level: When emotions fly high during a heated debate, for instance, one or both parties might feel as if their relationship level is worsening or being affected in a relatively negative manner. In this case, instead of presuming or conjecturing, we should stop and ask clarifying questions. Then we'll be better positioned to reduce the negative influence on a relationship level.

On an Emotional Level: Emotions can often be confusing because the same physical reaction covers several emotions. Crying, for instance, could be perceived as stemming from happiness, sadness, pain, etc. When one or both parties encounter an emotionally charged situation, and the nonverbal cues are confusing, it helps to ask clarifying questions to understand the emotional state and its cause.

Listening and Formulating Thoughts

Listening is a vital component of the communication process for the simple reason that verbal communication cannot be perceived through any other sense. So the key to receiving and interpreting communication is the effectiveness of our listening skills. As with most components of communication, listening is yet another skill that is not taught to us. It is something we learn and develop as we mature. Since there isn't any formal guidance, it is also a slow-developing skill, and often, we don't even realize that we're not fantastic at it.

The way we listen can be separated into three distinct categories:

Cosmetic: We could be looking directly at the speaker or the source of communication (television, for instance) and be utterly lost in our thoughts. This happens when a piece of incoming information triggers a chain of thoughts. For example, if the speaker were to use a food analogy in his speech, it might remind a listener that they hadn't quite figured out what they'd be making for dinner. From there, the listener might recall that the fridge and pantry were empty and basic groceries were required. The listener would then make a mental to-do list and continue not to be receptive to the speaker. In situations like this, we need to make a conscious effort to focus on the incoming communication rather than allowing ourselves to remain distracted. It is almost always noticeable when we're listening cosmetically. Remember the time the teacher unexpectedly called your name in class? Or the time when you thought you could sleep through a conference since you were not actively involved and no one would miss you, but then your boss turned the spotlight on you?

Conversational: This is the listening version of spoken destructive communication. Recall the example we discussed at the onset of this chapter. The two girls were involved in nonconstructive communication as each talked about what was on their minds. Neither connected with the other nor became part of the other's conversation. Similarly, in conversational listening, we listen, then deviate to a different subject when we speak, and the cycle continues.

Active: This is the ideal form of listening; one where the listener is completely engaged in the incoming communication—from receiving (via listening) to interpreting and processing nonverbal cues, returning nonverbal cues (nodding, smiling, etc.) to asking clarifying questions.

Active Listening Techniques and Strategies:

Ensure you have the right attitude—focus on the communication, and if you find yourself getting distracted, refocus your mind on the subject.

Be mindful of your nonverbal cues like facial expression, posture, and body position. Since the speaker relies on nonverbal cues to determine the communication's effectiveness, it is essential to ensure that we give out the correct nonverbal cues.

Avoid the barriers to constructive communication, like interrupting a speaker or presuming or conjecturing. Formulate your thoughts and wait for the appropriate moment to voice them.

If you happened to interrupt, help the speaker to recall where they stopped, and continue their flow of thoughts.

Inhale or count to five before you speak. That pause will help curb impulsiveness. This is most effective in situations where emotions run high. We become so emotionally charged that our mind starts working on counter arguments. We don't allow ourselves to continue receiving the communication and end up missing vital parts.

One of the things that distract us when receiving information is overly focusing on the speaker's features—be it their tone, gestures, appearance, mistakes, etc. Don't let these sidetrack you.

If it so happens that you find yourself in disagreement with the speaker right from the first sentence, don't close your mind. Be open and receptive; listen to them, and make an effort to consider their perspective. It does often happen that the speaker needs a little run-up before they make their point.

Make a conscious effort to remove distractions. Close curtains, switch off lights if they're too bright, or switch on lights if the room is too dim. Silence phones and close doors. Outside sounds and people entering and leaving mid-way through a speech, for instance, should be avoided.

Formulating and Articulating Thoughts

Just as it doesn't benefit a speaker to present jumbled thoughts and vague ideas, it doesn't help if the listener is ambiguous when they voice their opinions. One of the easiest ways to remain effective in our communication—both as a recipient and a speaker—is to keep messages short and simple. Revisit your thoughts and ideas and try to identify unnecessary elements. Anything that doesn't carry a vital meaning should be removed to maintain effectiveness.

It is also helpful to start with a brief list of the points you want to cover. A simple introduction along the lines of "I would like to speak about the attrition rates before discussing profit and loss" would help keep you on track.

This extra effort also prepares everyone present and gives them an added awareness of your direction. It will also allow the participants to redirect their focus, if it had shifted, to parts of your communication that they might have missed.

Don't be in a hurry. In today's fast-paced world, people have no patience for anything that takes more than a few seconds or minutes. Think of the most commonly typed text message—HRU? A longer than usual wait at a drive-thru would have us fuming. This constant focus on speed takes away from our thought formulation abilities. Intelligent arguments cannot be formed in a split second as there are just too many 'buts' and 'ifs' to consider. Take your time to organize your thoughts. Write them down if necessary.

If the situation allows for it, rehearse your communication/responses/clarifying questions. Pay attention to your delivery. Keep emotions in check and consider what emotions your words will trigger in your audience. You'll sound more sensible, credible, and confident if your communication is concise yet well drafted.

And finally, one of the earliest suggestions was to catch your listener's attention by making your message engaging. You can do so by switching from formal to informal and facts to storytelling.

Chapter 2 Part 2: Emotions and their Role in Communication

During a conversation, people exchange more than their thoughts and ideas. They also share emotions. Proper communication will always include a stable and healthy composition of emotions.

> "Why was I scolded?"
>
> "Why was she angry when I suggested that we manage our budget better."

These questions reflect our emotions or the emotional situations we share with people around us.

Emotions are a direct expression of how we relate to our environment, the people around us, and ourselves! Often, the memory of an occasion lasts longer because of the emotions we felt. This emotional memory also affects our future behavior. In most cases, people undergo significant behavioral changes after an incident with a tremendous emotional impact.

Emotions serve a biological purpose from a survival perspective. It marks events in our memory to preserve their significance. Connecting products to our emotions—

happiness, satisfaction, etc.—is a way to make commercials and advertisements memorable.

Regulation of Emotions

Emotions are a large part of our communication. It is advisable to understand how it affects communication efficiency. Positive emotions are not a cause for concern as they don't distort our messages. Negative emotions, however, influence our interaction process.

A Few Things to Remember

- Accept that emotions prevail in a conversation.

- Identify what emotions are surfacing in your communication.

- Analyze what situations or subjects or people trigger certain negative emotions.

- Get feedback on how you behave when your negative emotions take over.

- Analyze what consequences your reactions have.

- Finally, ask yourself if you're okay with the results of your emotional behavior.

If your answer was 'no,' then you need to focus on techniques that will help you to manage your emotions.

Chapter 3 Part 1: The Importance of Listening

One of the foremost means through which we learn new information is by listening. We engage in the listening process long before we start verbal or nonverbal communication. It is not an instinctive skill—it is learned, just like speaking, reading, and writing.

Why is Listening Important?

- It allows us to understand instructions, which invariably helps us complete tasks at home, school, or work.

- It also helps us recall, evaluate, and respond to messages.

- We listen to our partners and family members as it helps us meet our relationship needs as well.

- It allows us to receive and interpret verbal and nonverbal messages.

Self-concept, as we discussed in Effective Communication, grows with the perceptions people form about us. Listening allows us to communicate our identity needs and develop an accurate self-concept. Therefore, it comes as no surprise that listening is a crucial skill to develop if we want to grow as people and professionals and enhance the effectiveness of our communication skills.

The Listening Process

Like communication, the listening process has no start or end. And it doesn't work like a pipeline—there is no step-by-step process here. Several elements are enmeshed in the listening process—as with communication—including behavioral, emotional, and cognitive. The listening process does have several stages, though. Let's jump straight in!

1. The Receiving Stage

This is the first stage of the listening process as we intentionally focus on and prepare ourselves to hear the speaker's message. To do so requires us to filter out "noise," which, as explained in previous chapters, includes all the distractions that affect communication.

We listen with our ears—everyone knows that. But what most people don't realize is that we also listen with our eyes. As odd as that may be, it is true. Try walking around for a bit with your eyes closed. The world of sound would terrify you because you can't see the nonverbal cues you've come to rely on. Take, for instance, sarcasm. You can't tell if the speaker is sarcastic if they're saying something like,

"No, no, go ahead. Do that again," unless you see what their facial expressions are communicating as well.

So, listening is a skill duly supported by our other senses, as it gives us a broader overview of the nonverbal cues that help us interpret messages.

Ask yourself this. Are you more likely to have a miscommunication when speaking with someone in person or through technology (like email or chat)? Since visual clues are missing in technology-enabled communication, you're more likely to agree that email, chat, and phone conversations limit your contextual clues and present you with difficulties when trying to interpret interactions.

2. The Interpreting Stage

This is the stage where we combine visual and auditory information and try to make sense of that information. Of course, several factors either help us or limit our ability to make sense of communication. Take, for instance, a conversation in the middle of the street. The blaring horn of a passing vehicle will restrict our listening, and we won't quite grasp what was said to us.

3. The Recalling Stage

Recalling is a part of the listening process. If we've heard a message and focused on it, we're more likely to remember it. If, however, we were in part distracted during the receiving stage, we're less likely to remember the message or parts of it. There is a catch, though. Even when we're paying complete attention to a form of communication, our ability to remember that message depends on its simplicity or complexity.

4. The Evaluating Stage

This is a complex stage wherein we make judgments about a message and/or the speaker.

- We need to decide whether the speaker is credible.

- We need to judge the completeness of the communication.

- We need to assess nonverbal cues and attach meaning to the message based on the signals.

- Equally important is the "worth" we assign to the message. Good or bad, right or wrong—these are some of the categories in which we "fit" messages.

Critical thinking skills are imperative for this stage of the listening process. Without critical thinking, not only will we be unable to evaluate messages and communications, but we'll also find ourselves limited in our participation in the communication process.

Think back to the time where you almost fell asleep during a lecture or a conference. How productive did you feel? What was your contribution to the discussion?

5. The Responding Stage

When we're passive listeners, we are unable to make sense of the communication. Equally, we're unable to retain most of what we might have heard. This affects our ability to respond. A passive listener's lack of nonverbal and verbal cues, of course, is a form of feedback to the speaker. Note-taking, head nodding, clarifying doubts, prompting questions that lead to new discussions—these are the verbal and nonverbal cues that speakers rely on to gauge their audience's reaction and decide whether to change their attitude and approach. For instance, the speaker can switch from formal to the informal style of speech and vice versa.

Chapter 3 Part 2: Listening Types

Just as there are different stages in the listening process, there are different types of listening. Since listening serves many functions, we tend to employ a different type of skill depending on the situation. For example, the listening type we use when in a classroom or conference room will be hugely different from the listening type we use in a social context.

What are the Types of Listening?

Discriminative

Imagine this scenario: You're sitting in a rocking chair on your porch, enjoying a hot cup of tea after a particularly heavy dinner. As you gently rock back and forth, you hear a sound. You stop rocking and strain or wait to hear if the sound repeats. Could it be the dog in the yard? A creepy-crawly on a bush nearby? Could a loose wooden plank on your porch have contributed to the sound? Or could the sound be an indication of something dangerous? Perhaps it's the cougar you heard about in the news earlier.

When we focus our hearing to isolate and process a specific kind of sound, we're employing discriminative listening. In the above situation, we're listening for sounds, and in the absence of visual stimuli, we're assigning meaning to the communication. Discriminative listening tends to be physiological and occurs at the receiving stage. It is an instrumental type of listening that allows us to isolate auditory or visual stimuli and scan and monitor our surroundings. It dictates how we respond to specific communication. For example, if a co-worker were to sound 'sad' while trying to impress on you that they're all right, you might press them to be honest. You're displaying concern and being approachable, which in turn might earn the co-worker's trust and encourage them to ask you for help.

Informational

This type of listening is best exemplified with examples of everyday activities such as hearing voice messages; listening to news reports, briefings at work, instructions, or directions when we're traveling; and in a classroom or university context. Here, our objective is to understand and retain the information being presented to us. This is not an evaluative form of listening. If we don't employ informational listening, then we won't be able to perform the most basic of tasks, be it in a social, academic, personal, or professional context.

Critical

Imagine this scenario: You've just finished your holiday season binge only to realize you cannot fit into your favorite pants. Now what? You scour for quick and effective weight loss solutions. You come across one fascinating proposal. Drink this solution in the morning and at night and lose five pounds; no exercise required. Sounds good? Perhaps too good. Wouldn't obesity be eliminated if such a miracle solution actually existed? And so, you move on to another suggestion.

Why? What made you decide that the first proposal wasn't worth your time?

When we stop to evaluate communication presented to us in verbal form, we're employing critical listening skills. At this stage of the listening process, we're determining whether the information and speaker are credible and whether the message has faulty logic. When we're not convinced, we don't jump to speculating and conjecturing; instead, we move to the clarifying question stage of effective communication. With the tech boom, we have so many communication platforms that consumers are bombarded with messages. Critical thinking and listening are crucial skills to develop.

Empathetic

Imagine this conversation:

> Supervisor: We had agreed to a deliverable for today. Why hasn't it been sent?

> Employee: My apologies, but my mother-in-law passed in the early morning hours, and I have been unable to work as scheduled. Can we shift the delivery to tomorrow, please?
>
> Supervisor: No, I want the delivery today.
>
> Employee: But I have hospital obligations and funeral details to sort.
>
> Supervisor: Manage it during your personal hours. Work needs to be completed during office hours.

Ouch, right? Who'd want to work with a supervisor like that? And what would a conversation like that do to the relationship between the supervisor and the employee? And what if other employees overheard this conversation?

Sympathy and Empathy are often used interchangeably. However, they're not the same. A sympathetic boss would say, "I'm sorry to hear about your loss, but I need that done by today."

An empathetic boss, however, would say, "I'm sorry to hear about your loss. Take the bereavement time you need. I will reassign that task to someone else."

Empathetic listening involves putting yourself in the other person's situation and relating to their experience, and then determining the best response for that scenario. It requires open-mindedness and civility. Empathetic listening is crucial to forming and maintaining interpersonal relationships.

Listening skills are not taught to us, either. It is yet another communication skill that we develop as we grow. And our culture and experiences affect what kind of listeners we become. Here's a quick look at the different categories we can divide listeners into based on their listening style:

- **People-oriented-** listeners who get distracted from a message or task because they focus on addressing feelings. They focus on the message to figure out what the speaker is thinking or feeling instead of considering that the message is about something that the speaker considers important.

- **Action-oriented-** listeners who get frustrated easily when communication is perceived as unorganized or inconsistent. They are interested in learning what the speaker wants. The faster the speaker makes their point, the better. They prefer compelling messages over underlying reasons.

- **Content-oriented-** listeners who enjoy complex messages and prefer as much detail as you can offer. They spend a lot of time and energy deciding whether the message is accurate, whether the speaker is credible, and what the message means. If the message is too brief or lacks sufficient supporting data, it will sound like an infomercial to a content-oriented listener. Solid information, plenty of explanations, and well-developed information are important to content-oriented listeners.

- **Time-oriented-** listeners who are task-oriented and prefer concisely communicated information. Lengthy messages usually earn time-oriented listener's impatience. They are prone to using nonverbal cues to express their impatience. They will tune out, fidget, or multitask when messages are too long.

The Challenge of Listening

Noise, as we know, is any unwanted stimuli or signal that affects an incoming message or communication. Noise is detrimental to effective communication as it distorts the message. For communication to be efficient, the recipient must receive the message as the sender intended.

Multitasking is a criterion for survival in our fast-paced world. Doing several things at once has become such an integral part of our lives that we no longer notice that we're doing it, and we certainly don't see its pitfalls. Anything that forces our brains to process multiple incoming communications invariably leads to lowered performance and a higher likelihood of miscommunication—whether we're willing to accept it or not.

Consider a few scenarios:

Your mom calls while you're reading an important email. You answer the phone, expecting her to talk about her day as usual. You find yourself going, "Yeah, yeah, okay, fine...wait, what did you say? Uncle Sam died? When did that happen? Why didn't you tell me before? No, I'd have remembered it had you told me that." And in the silence that follows, you can feel your mother rolling her eyes at you.

You walk into the living room and give your spouse a verbal shopping list. Your spouse looks at you, nods, and then goes back to watching television. An hour later, your spouse approaches you in the kitchen and says, "I'm heading out. Do you want anything from the store?" And such a situation would cause you to mutter, "You never listen when I speak."

Managing several forms of media together is called media multitasking. It can positively and negatively impact our ability to listen. Why? Because media multitasking interferes with listening at its various stages. Let's see how.

- **Receiving stage-** noise can block or distort incoming communication. Remember the time you were listening to music and couldn't hear your parents call you?

- **Interpreting stage-** noise makes it difficult to understand complex or abstract information. Remember when you checked your messages during a lecture and then found it difficult to understand what the professor was teaching?

- **Recalling stage-** noise and subsequent distractions challenge our concentration and interfere with our recollection abilities. Such as when the professor asked you to read from the textbook, and you couldn't remember where he had stopped.

- **Evaluating stage-** noise in the form of personal biases and prejudices can prompt us to interrupt the speaker or block them out completely.

- **Responding stage-** we become passive listeners when our attention is divided, owing to which, we lack comprehension of an incoming communication. This can cause misunderstandings as we don't have the subject level knowledge to paraphrase and ask clarifying questions.

What are Some of the Barriers to Listening?

Environmental Factors

Several environmental factors, such as temperature and light, affect our listening abilities. A room that's too dark makes us sleepy, while a space that's too bright makes us uncomfortable and distracts us. When a room is too cold or hot, it creates physical discomfort that diverts our attention from the speaker. If you haven't eaten enough, you might just focus on how hungry you're feeling instead of listening to the speaker. Physical injuries or ailments and our mood can also affect our listening abilities. Physical noise is another factor that interferes with listening. Construction noises, loud music, etc. Semantic noise can also cause a listener to lose focus. When you struggle to interpret the speaker's message, you get left behind on a subject level.

Cognitive and Personal Barriers

We fail to understand messages that are too complex. Since comfort with complexity levels varies from person to person, the onus to study the audience and change lies with the speaker. Media multitasking is a perfect example of how cognitive barriers affect our listening. We focus on too many things at once, or we're always thinking about all the things we need to do later (check Facebook, make that Instagram post, the online multiplayer game that we need to log into, etc.). This reduces our receptiveness toward incoming communication.

Personal barriers could include our general attitude toward listening. The 21st century is a noise-driven society. Literally, not figuratively. People want to speak, and they want the whole world as their audience. Everyone is clamoring over everyone else for their turn to speak. When everyone is communicating all at once, who is left to listen? And what are our patience levels, and how receptive are we to others' communication when we're impatient?

Speech and Thought Rate Factor

Remember that family member or friend who rattles on like an out-of-control train, and you just can't keep up with them? Humans think and process information much faster than our speech rate—think 800 words a minute (thoughts) and 175 words a minute (speech). Is it a wonder why we find ourselves daydreaming or distracted by thoughts that don't match the speaker's communication at a subject level.

Attention Span

Attention span is another contributing factor. When we're addressing children, we tend to remember that they have short attention spans. However, adults are expected to not only have longer attention spans, but to also regulate themselves and overcome superficial issues. Most speakers forget that attention is finite.

Ineffective Speakers

Remember the complexity argument? Communication senders are liable for more than just the complexity of the communication they send. They lose the listeners' attention when messages are poorly constructed, when they're too vague, or even too simple. Barriers also crop up when their delivery fails. Verbal fillers, monotone voices, appearance, and even their nonverbal cues can distract a listener.

Openness

When we are convinced of an idea or thought, we tend to be close-minded to others' suggestions. We begin the conversation without the openness required to make us receptive to communication. We listen, but on a superficial or aggressive level where our goal or aim is to preserve our ways of thinking.

Apprehension

Most people, especially in an academic or professional context, fear their inability to understand messages or absorb information coherently. This is easily identifiable, if for instance, a student intentionally avoids a certain course or lecture.

Listening Practices that Affect Communication.

The above-mentioned barriers to effective listening could prove challenging to overcome as they are partially beyond our control. Despite the conscious effort we make to lessen these barriers' impact, we have to accept that limitations and biases exist within us and that we can't eliminate them.

What we can change, and with greater degrees of success, are the bad listening habits that we practice.

Eavesdropping

Intentionally listening to other people's conversations (eavesdropping) is not the same as walking into a room and overhearing someone's conversation. We're prone to eavesdrop when our curiosity overshadows our conscience. Eavesdropping is a bad listening habit—one that we must avoid regardless of how curious we are. It's better to approach the person and be honest with them.

Aggressive Listening

We employ aggressive listening habits when we want to attack the speaker even before they've spoken. This kind of listening goes hand-in-hand with conjecture. Here, we feel we know what the speaker is going to say, we are convinced that it is wrong, and we're ready with our reasons to oppose the idea and the speaker even before the first word is said. To avoid being aggressive listeners, we need to be patient and open-minded. Even if we have prejudices and biases, we must learn to hear the communication completely and openly before we oppose it.

Narcissistic Listening

When people often make every conversation about themselves or try to compete with the speaker at every available opportunity, it is considered narcissistic listening. Consider the following example.

> **Person A:** My landlord has been troubling me a lot lately. Now that our rent agreement is ending, he's demanding more money than we agreed to previously. With how terrible work has been, I don't know how I'll find the time to search for another apartment.
>
> **Person B:** That's not so bad. You have no idea what I have to live with. My boss is nuts. My colleagues are incompetent. I'm trying to work toward my degree, but my partner keeps whining that I don't give enough attention at home.

While it may seem as though Person B is contributing to the conversation, Person B is, in essence, shifting the attention to himself. To avoid becoming narcissistic listeners, we need to time our interruptions more carefully.

Types of Listening Responses

Listening response is the way we respond to communication (keeping in mind that most communication is verbal). There are several types of listening responses, and these can vary from silent listening to evaluating to advising.

Silent Listening

A child walks up to a parent and says, "May I please play on the computer?" The parent glares at the child in silence instead of replying. The child slinks away with the understanding that they've done something wrong or undesirable.

It's acceptable to remain silent in some situations—think about lectures or briefings where we need to gather information. When used correctly, our silence can be more powerful than our words. However, when we misjudge the situation and use silence as a response, we could give the wrong impression.

Questioning

Humans are curious, and curiosity leads to questions. Questioning is a typical listening response, but only when we're listening actively. Passive listeners can be identified by their lack of questioning. To avoid giving the wrong impression, we need to monitor the way we question (tone) and how we word our questions. We can appear insolent if our tone is too aggressive. We can also appear presumptive; for example, if someone asks, "Tell me how often you've stolen from me."

Paraphrasing

Paraphrasing is an indicator of mindful listening. It shows the speaker that we were paying attention. We typically use paraphrasing when we need to verify information before we reach conclusions. "Correct me if I misunderstood you. But did you just say that...?"

Empathizing

We use this kind of listening response when we need to convey our understanding, be civil, and offer support. Statements usually begin with "I understand," "I'm so sorry for," etc.

When we deny someone else's feelings and pass judgment, we're not empathizing. Our response usually begins with "That's not a big deal" (or something similar) in such situations.

Analyzing

Just as we think critically and listen critically, we also analyze as a listening response. In such situations, our goal is to convey our interpretation of a speaker's message. Our interpretations often rest on the speaker's background knowledge or the message's context.

Evaluating

Evaluations are of two kinds—positive and negative. We tend to offer positive evaluations in situations where we're convinced of someone else's suggestions. Think of the times you've said "That sounds about right" or "That makes sense."

Negative evaluations can be further divided into two categories—judgment (most often accompanied by derogatory statements) and constructive (feedback, appraisals, etc.).

Advising

Advice can be an effective and valuable listening response. However, as with any listening response, you first want to ensure that it's the correct response in a given situation. Before giving advice, ask yourself the following questions:

- Is the advice needed?

- Is the advice wanted?

- Is the advice given in the proper order?

- Are you a close friend or someone the speaker trusts?

- Will you make the speaker feel as though you're supportive?

Chapter 4: Emotions

What are Emotions?

Emotions are complex feelings that bring about changes in thoughts and behaviors. They are caused by outside stimuli or physiological (body) changes. Since emotions are central to any interpersonal relationship, it is crucial to understand what causes and influences emotions. That way, we'll better understand our feelings and respond to others' display of emotions.

There are three components or key elements of emotions: subjective experience, a physiological response, and expressive response.

Elements of Emotions

Subjective Experience

Different people react to situations and stimuli differently. An event or stimuli that makes one person happy might not evoke the same feelings in another person.

Take a horror flick, for example.

- Some will be terrified by it and will have nightmares for a while. Eventually, they'll forget about it.

- Others are affected on a different level. Did a friend or family member develop a fear of spiders, snakes, or water after watching a related movie?

- Others will laugh through the movie and shrug off any effects or supposedly terrifying thoughts or ideas communicated through the film.

In all of these cases, the stimuli's effect on experience is subjective.

We have broad labels for emotions, and often several emotions are expressed similarly. For instance, if someone is angry, they will shout. If someone is annoyed or frustrated, they may raise their tone. There is a fine line that differentiates anger from frustration. Crying is another example. We cry when we're hurt (emotionally and physically) and when we're happy. To the recipient, however, these displays of emotions are confusing and subjective.

Mixed emotions are also a contributing factor to the subjective nature of our experiences. For instance, having a baby is a joyful moment, but the thought of parenthood also leaves us anxious. When we feel multiple emotions simultaneously or consecutively within a short span, it contributes to our experience's subjective nature.

Physiological Response

- Tears of joy and relief
- Heart palpitations
- Breaking out in a sweat

What do these have in common? No, they aren't examples of figurative speech. They're all actual physiological responses that we feel when our emotions are intense.

Behavioral Response

When we experience a situation that evokes an intense emotion, we are bound to express what we feel. A smile, a frown, raised tone, etc., are some of the nonverbal cues that indicate our emotional state.

Emotions and Communication

As with all other aspects of communication, learning to read emotions is something that we do unaided. It is not taught to us. However, we do receive explicit guidance during our growing years. Think of the times we've heard or given instructions like 'smile when you greet someone' or 'boys don't cry.' Emotion sharing involves communicating the circumstance, thoughts, and feelings that we feel after an emotional event. We learn to read emotions through trial and error. We spend most of our lives interpreting the emotional expressions of friends, family members, our office colleagues and seniors, and even strangers.

When we display or communicate (verbally) our emotions, we provide information to others that helps them decide how they should react. For instance, when we see someone we care about displaying behaviors related to sadness, we know that we need to offer support. When we can understand and interpret emotions correctly, we're said to have high emotional intelligence levels.

We've discussed how recipients interpret messages, attach meaning, and even make assumptions based on nonverbal cues. The inability to correctly match emotion with a verbal response would interfere with the recipient's ability to decode and interpret.

As with most communication aspects, we increase our emotion reading and interpreting competence with increased effort and knowledge. Our efficiency as communicators also increases when we have a greater awareness of how we experience and express emotions.

While emotions are often 'displayed' through nonverbal cues, humans can also express emotions verbally. Before we do so, we need to develop an emotional vocabulary. As with all aspects of communication, the more specific we are when we verbally express our emotions, the lower the likelihood of a misinterpretation by the person decoding our message.

A third way to communicate our emotions is through writing. This form has distinct advantages, such as allowing us the time to compose ourselves and our thoughts before we convey them to others. Thus, we're less likely to write something impulsive or harsh, which we'll regret at a later stage. There are disadvantages as well, as we cannot include significant context and nonverbal communication. For example, facial expressions and tone of voice. These nonverbal cues offer greater insight into emotions than is possible from written or verbal communication.

Another drawback is the lack of immediate feedback. How often have we sent emails or text messages to others and not received a response for hours, and sometimes, even days? Waiting for someone to respond negatively affects our emotional state, and subsequently, our relationship with the other person.

Purpose of Emotions

Emotions help us manage the complexities of our social life (interpersonal relations). When we share our emotions, we create understanding. By regulating how we share our feelings, we manage conflict. By showing empathy, we increase our interpersonal bond with other people.

How we express our emotions depends on our socio-cultural norms and rules. For example, people are expected to be more positive in the USA. In Japan, it is unacceptable to show fear in front of a superior. For cross-cultural communication to be effective, it is essential to understand socio-cultural norms and how and why emotions are or aren't displayed.

Role of Emotions

Emotions Motivate Us.

Consider this scenario: A work deadline is approaching, and you aren't quite done with your task. You'll feel anxious, and that will motivate you to work faster and endeavor to meet the deadline. Because you felt this particular emotion, you were encouraged to take action that would result in a positive. Next time around, you'll avoid some of the things that led to the situation, and you'll perhaps be better organized and prepared.

We're conditioned to see happiness. We tend to do all that is within our power to avoid situations that lead to negative emotions. The person you avoid speaking to, the road you won't travel by, the food you love eating, and the social activities you prefer following are some of the choices we make to get and maintain a sense of happiness and excitement.

Emotions Help Us Survive.

A walk down a strange, creepy alley is considered a risky venture. Jumping out of planes or freefalling from heights is considered madness (the adrenalin junkies will disagree with me here, but insurance companies are more likely to side with me). Eating food well past its expiration date is a suggestion that would cause you to hesitate. Going back to a restaurant where you got food poisoning is not something you'd consider. You get the idea. The instinct to remain safe, to preserve life, to survive—whatever you choose to call it—comes from a "fear" of something, and it keeps us from taking certain risks. It maximizes our survival and success chances.

Emotions Help with Decisions.

Didn't enjoy oatmeal for breakfast? Go "ahh" with that steaming hot cup of coffee? Frustration with the nuances of public transport pushed you to buy a car? See where we're headed? It isn't just the "practicalities" of things or situations that prompt you to make certain decisions. Your emotions also guide you. Do keep in mind that intense moments that evoke powerful emotions may lead to poor decision-making.

Emotion Works Both Ways When it Comes to Understanding.

Just as we cue into others' emotions during a communication exchange to help us interpret their message, others will analyze and process our nonverbal cues to understand what emotions we're experiencing. This "emotion" exchange is crucial as it allows both sides to decide what course of action needs to be taken. Emotional expressions are a wealth of information, and how proficiently we interpret and react to the cues we see will build or destroy our social relationships.

The depth and intensity of the emotions we feel are dependent on our subjective experience. For instance, an unexpected ending to a movie will leave us feeling dissatisfied for a short period. However, a friend's betrayal could have us reeling for a much longer time. Developing higher emotional intelligence will help us manage our emotions better and respond to others' emotions effectively. Since how communication is decoded (interpreted) lies in the speaker's nonverbal cues, the ability to read emotions will help us succeed when we communicate with other people. More often than not, understanding how a person is communicating is more important than what they say.

Four Ways to Improve Your Emotional Awareness

1. Consider Others' Feelings

Ever walked up to someone and asked them a question only to have them snap back at you? Confused about what you might have said or done to merit that reaction? Did that reaction cause you to be bitter in your response? Take a moment to reconsider your interpretation of the situation. Perhaps that person was tense or frustrated about something else and subconsciously communicated it to you. Asking clarifying questions in this scenario will help us figure out what that person is trying to tell you. Pay attention to that emotion and not the message.

2. Empathy

Once you've figured out what the other person is feeling, you can go a step further and relate to their feelings. By putting yourself in their situation, you'll figure out how to speak to that person and what to say.

3. Consider Your Feelings

Just as messages are affected by other peoples' feelings, your communication is affected by your feelings. More often than not, feelings get in the way of communication.

Focus on your emotions before you communicate to avoid the risk of misinterpretation.

4. Trust

Think back to how we determine the credibility of a speaker. In much the same way, we build credibility and trust with others—our nonverbal cues should match our verbal communication. What would you think of a person's message if they were to say 'yes' but shake their head? What if the person were to say they're okay but do so with a frown or a glare?

Conflict between verbal and nonverbal cues also leads to misunderstandings. By developing or enhancing your emotional awareness, you'll reduce the opportunities for misunderstandings. You could walk away when someone snaps at you for no identifiable reason, but you'll be troubled by why and assume it's something you did. Assumptions or conjectures like that will affect the relationship you have with that person.

Guidelines for Expressing Emotions

The way we express our emotions is dictated by our cultural, familial, and socio-economic backgrounds. Even gender plays a role in how we express our emotions. For instance, women are more attuned to feelings, and they have a stronger, more intense reaction to situations. They, thus, have a more extensive range of feelings. On the other hand, men reveal more positive feelings and often find it easier to share emotions with women than with other men. Social conventions are another determining factor in how we communicate our emotions. For instance, in collectivistic cultures, members avoid direct conflict situations. In individualistic cultures, people focus more on themselves and their needs. They, however, have a low-context communication technique. That being said, universal rules apply to almost every form of interaction, including how we express our emotions.

Here is a set of guidelines that will make expressing emotions relatively conflict-free.

- Accept and value your feelings. Everyone has them. Instead of ignoring emotions, it is better to express them.

- Identify your feelings. Emotions can be confusing. For example, anger can feel like frustration. However, they are not the same. The intensity of emotions also varies. Emotions aren't always expressed verbally. They are, therefore, easier to identify based on physiological changes that you feel.

- When you express your feelings, try to be specific instead of ambiguous or general. Use phrases like "I feel" to guide you.

- Specify the degree or intensity of your feelings as well—a little irritated, very irritated, absolutely fuming. Develop an emotional vocabulary so that you can avoid being misunderstood.

- If your emotions are overpowering, take a little time to calm down. Often, we get carried away with our emotions and say things we invariably regret.

- Remember to describe the behavior or situational context that led to powerful emotions. Without that, the other person cannot identify or figure out what went wrong.

- It helps to use "I" sentences. When using "You" sentences, the recipient will feel like they're being attacked. Instead of understanding, they'll start defending themselves, and the issue will escalate.

- Be respectful of people and boundaries.

- Try to highlight the positives. "I am thankful for...but I am upset about..."

- Be mindful of your nonverbal cues. It doesn't help if you say you're a little upset about something, but your tone or facial expression indicates that the severity of your emotion is well above what you've expressed verbally.

Learning to express emotion safely and in a non-aggressive manner takes time and patience. Enlist the support of others you trust to help you identify your strengths and shortcomings.

Managing and Responding to Emotions

Imagine this scenario: your friend just got an expensive gift that she's been coveting for a while. She's excited and calls you to share her emotions. You reply with, "Yeah, okay. That's great. I'm happy for you."

What would your friend feel when she hears that robotic response?

Engaging in emotion sharing is a two-way experience. When someone shares an emotional event with us, we find ourselves at the receiving end. But the process doesn't stop there. By understanding and interpreting their emotions, we decide the best way for us to return that communication. This adaptability is crucial to building interpersonal relationships. Just as you wouldn't reply robotically to your friend's excitement, you wouldn't sound happy or enthusiastic when someone tells you that they're having a terrible day.

When people communicate or express emotions, they expect results that can range from support to advice and even validation. Remember the time a friend shared that they'd lost a family member? Awkward and unsure of what to say, your response came in the form of a hug. While you may feel inadequate for being unable to offer appropriate comforting words, the hug was perhaps powerful enough to console your friend. Being at the receiving end of emotional sharing is challenging for most of us. But with persistent effort, understanding (emotions and their effect on communication), and feedback from others (on our responses to emotional communication), we can enhance our communication competence.

Chapter 5: Dynamics of Interpersonal Relationships

Human evolution over millions of years has shown that our interpersonal relationships and communication developed as we grew into a more cohesive society. Had we lived alone instead of in close-knit groups, we'd have no reason to develop such advanced communication skills, nor would we worry so much about the relationships we form and what we must do to maintain them. Just as living in isolation led to lowered survival chances for early humans, maintaining social bonds and living in groups resulted in better adaptability to stress, greater satisfaction in relationships, a wider network, and lowered depression and anxiety levels.

Is it a wonder that interpersonal communication skills are highly sought after by employers?

What is Interpersonal Communication?

While communication is the process of exchanging messages between a sender and a recipient, interpersonal communication adds the element of 'relationships.' What this means is that you're not a stranger waving a greeting at another passing stranger. On the contrary, for a meaningful exchange to be defined as interpersonal, it must be with someone you know—your family, friends, partner, etc. Interpersonal also extends to communication between two or more people who can significantly influence each other because of a unique bond.

We often find ourselves challenged by our interpersonal communication skills, just like all other forms of communication discussed earlier. To make the most of our relationships, we must understand and follow some basic principles.

Goal-oriented

We ought to be strategic when it comes to interpersonal communication. Why? Because each interpersonal communication has a goal to meet. And so, we must create messages with which to achieve our goals. The more effective our communication, the greater the likelihood that we'll attain our objective. These goals are necessary as they help us function in our relationships.

Our goals are not static. On the contrary, they change depending on the situation and our needs. If you find that you struggle with achieving your goal after a conversation, you know that you cannot communicate effectively in your relationships.

Appropriate vs. Effective

Micromanagement in a professional or social context is a perfect example of situations where we struggle to manage or prioritize appropriateness and effectiveness.

Let's consider an example from a social context.

A mother asks her child to clean her room. Once the communication happens and the child understands what is expected of her, the mother can do one of two things.

> a) She supervises, criticizes, and instructs.

> b) She leaves and trusts the child to decide what needs cleaning and what doesn't.

In the first instance, the room will be cleaned as per the mother's expectations. Effectiveness achieved. However, what impact does this form of micromanagement have on the child?

In the second instance, the room is cleaned as per the child, which may not have met the mother's goals. However, given the more positive impact on the child, it would have been a more suitable approach.

Most people are uncomfortable with such a degree of micromanagement. To be competent interpersonal communicators, we must identify what is important to us—

goals or appropriateness—and then pick our communication accordingly.

The Two Aspects of Interpersonal Communication

1. Functional

Relationships are forged because they serve a need. Think of the different relationships you have and try to identify what 'need' each serves. Even if we aren't as self-centered and calculated as that statement makes us sound, we make an effort to grow relationships depending on the 'need' each serves.

Let's consider some examples.

- Leaving work early to attend your spouse's birthday party will serve as a relationship-maintenance goal.

- Calling your friend and asking them to help you shift your furniture over a weekend is an example of communication with an instrumental goal.

- Working overtime at a new job would be an example of a self-presentation goal. The intent is to portray yourself as a serious and dedicated employee.

2. Cultural

Relationship cultures are created through interpersonal communication. When we say culture, we mean the language and rituals that develop between people on a smaller, group-level scale. Two family members agreeing to a weekly phone call, for instance, is a relationship cultural ritual. Such cultural rituals, languages, and even values are unique to the partners in that relationship. The culture we follow on a societal level forms the basis or building blocks of the culture we establish on a relationship level.

Shared experiences build and strengthen relationships. Two classmates who didn't get along in school might reconnect at a reunion several decades later and laugh over the physics teacher's eccentricities. Two friends separated by oceans meet after a long time, overcome the initial awkwardness they feel by recounting the time they went whitewater rafting. In this case, storytelling served the purpose of creating or reinforcing a sense of closeness through a shared experience. Deciding which partner cooks on weekdays or weekends, which one does the house chores or the grocery shopping, establishes relationship routines that lend predictability and stability to relationships.

Conflict and Interpersonal Communication

Conflict is an inevitable part of life. Every interaction that we have on a personal, professional, or social level has the potential to end in conflict.

- A couple arguing over which type of car to purchase.
- Colleagues at loggerheads over shared tablespace.
- Siblings quarreling over estate or property division.

Sometimes, conflict is expressed verbally, and sometimes, warnings of an impending conflict are detected from nonverbal cues. Think glares, extended periods of silence, cold shoulder treatment, etc. Conflict, in itself, is not a negative. In fact, conflict can be productive. However, most people grow to fear it. This is because of how we handle conflict.

Conflict doesn't need to be emotionally exhausting, and it doesn't have to carry a negative connotation. Our efficiency as communicators rests on how we handle (not avoid) conflict and whether or not we attain a desirable result. For most of us, relief comes in the form of Human Resource teams (at work). But what about other aspects of our lives?

Handling conflicts in a productive manner can make life more pleasant. It is certainly not advisable to let the situation stagnate as the adverse effects of a conflict can quickly escalate from awkwardness or passive-aggressive comments to employment termination. The negative impact of conflict escalation is much more severe (think violence, loss of life, etc.).

Unfortunately, there is no clear set of rules that guide us as we navigate through conflicts. That being said, there are conflict management styles. Learning more about the conflict management styles and their advantages and disadvantages can help us determine what kind suits us and how we can adapt and become better at such a crucial skill.

Conflict Management Styles

There are five strategies for managing conflict. But before we jump into them, let's first try to identify your conflict management style.

- Do you dislike conflict and go out of your way to avoid it?

- Do you speak and rationalize till you get your way?

- Do your peers praise your ability to settle awkward situations through understanding and compromise?

- Are you known to invest a lot of time and effort into resolving a conflict?

Chances are you've been able to identify situations where each of those questions would apply. How is it that we can already be knowledgeable about different ways to navigate through conflict, and as equipped as we may be, we see varying results? Context is everything when managing conflict. Our decision on how to resolve a dispute rests entirely on how we see ourselves and how we see others in the context of the situation that led to the clash.

Elements of the Five Strategies for Managing Conflict

Competing

Let's consider a scenario. Two parents argue over an appropriate Christmas budget for their child. The issue settles when they agree to not go beyond $200. During the subsequent shopping trip, the mother finds that the father has broken the agreement by allowing the child to purchase something that crossed $200. While this may seem commonplace—we've all been there and done that—there is a deeper significance. Here, the man has low regard for his wife and strives to win by taking an indirect route. He's competing in a way that would help him get his way.

Avoiding

Continuing with the above scenario: the wife, upon noticing what her husband has done, rolls her eyes, and passes a sarcastic comment. She did not directly confront him; she chose to avoid the conflict altogether. However, she used verbal and nonverbal cues to display what she was feeling. The friction from before surfaced, but it wasn't addressed as she gave no input. That means it will fester and escalate till it blows out of proportion at a later time.

Sometimes, certain situations merit avoidance. Consider the time you ignored the rude driver who chose to lean on his horn way more than was necessary. Your parents are visiting for a day or a week, and you've sworn to avoid rising to your mother's persistent efforts to convince you it's time to get married and have babies because you know you aren't getting any younger.

Most times, however, avoidance only means the conflict will simmer and bleed into other situations.

Accommodating

Imagine if your mother sat down next to you with an album filled with photographs and bios of all the eligible men she knew. Most likely, they are related to someone from her crochet and bingo group. What would you do? You know she won't rest till you've read each one. And so, you call off your dinner plans, grab some coffee, stifle that yawn, and oblige by sitting as she flips the pages and oohs and aahs.

The accommodating style is often seen as passive or submissive. However, its appropriateness and effectiveness rest entirely on the context and our motivation.

Compromising

Consider this scenario. Your spouse is offered their dream job in a different city. It is only natural to be hesitant or to have concerns. You sit and talk it all out and eventually move. One day, you and your partner are discussing plans for an upcoming long weekend. He suggests visiting his parents. You lament, "You said I could visit my mother every month. I haven't seen her in two months. Now we're spending weekends with your parents. What about my mother? I knew we should never have agreed to move."

An outcome that requires a compromise isn't always a good thing. This is evident from people's efforts to seek out the positive from that compromise. It's a win-win situation, they tell themselves, with the hopes that they'll accept the outcome despite what they had to give up. What's wrong with that? Everything. While it may seem as though the compromise resolved the conflict, it was only temporary. People eventually focus on what they didn't get, and that leads to resentment and regret.

Collaborating

We've all faced it often enough. You know, the situation where a team deadline is missed. Everyone put in long hours and carried their weight. Some carried others as well.

And yet, the outcome was not as expected. So now what? The entire team sits down and discusses all the things that went right and all the things that went wrong, without pointing fingers or assigning blame. There's no scapegoat needed. It's a team effort, and the consequences are to be carried by the whole team.

From the junior trainee to the senior-most team member, everyone, even the department manager, gets to voice their opinions and suggestions—as equals. A plan is made, and everyone agrees. That's collaborating. An efficient problem-solving way of creating a win-win situation that assures mutual benefits and satisfaction. Bonus? It strengthened the teams' overall relationship.

Every individual has different growing experiences and influences such as culture that affect the development of their communication competence. Not everyone engaging in a conversation or working toward conflict resolution has the same knowledge and understanding of 'how to.' Fortunately, it only takes one person with the skills to make an interaction effective.

Negotiation Steps

The process of trying to change or influence conditions within a specific scenario is called negotiation. We negotiate every day. We may negotiate with a friend over activities, with a colleague over tasks, or a professor over an assignment. Negotiation has several stages that range from pre-negotiation to opening to settlement.

Pre-negotiation

When there's a conflict-like situation, it's best to prepare both sides for the ensuing discussion. This is the pre-negotiation stage. By setting a date or time for this discussion, both sides will have the opportunity to consider the conflict and what result they'd like to see. Instead of walking up to a person and blindsiding them with, "Hey, you didn't do the dishes like you were supposed to," and instantly put them on the defensive, it works to everyone's advantage if you say something like, "I've noticed that you've been busy lately. Can we discuss chore distribution when you have a few minutes?"

When another person doesn't do what they were supposed to and it affects us, frustration and annoyance arise. These emotions are evident in our tone when we confront the other person. While it is essential to share our feelings, a frustrated or annoyed tone is likely to be reciprocated by the other person. When entering a discussion, it helps to be pleasant.

Choice of words is equally important during the pre-negotiation stage. It never helps to use upsetting words (like name-calling) and accusations (you always do...). "I" statements work best as they don't make the other person feel like they're being judged.

Exploration

This is the stage during which both sides see and understand the conflict from a holistic perspective. The objective isn't to assign blame. Leave ego and pride aside. Consider it a high-level information exchange. Most people aren't aware that a conflict-like situation is building until they're confronted. Resentment and anger build up over time, especially if one person tried to avoid addressing the conflict when it first arose. It is important to check emotions, speak in a neutral tone, and listen actively. Once you've aired your concerns, it is vital to allow the other person to speak and put forward their case. This is essential—the objective of any negotiation is to resolve a situation based on mutual understanding. It will not work or be a negotiation if our objective is to "get our way."

Bargaining

When the discussion reaches this stage, both sides will have proposals in mind to help address the situation. One or both sides may even ask for concessions. Flexibility is crucial, as you might learn new information during the exploration stage that will influence your ideal outcome. Proposals put forward should not sound like ultimatums such as, if you don't, then I will.

Settlement

Everyone should be clear about and have the same understanding of the terms reached in the bargaining stage. It helps to lay out clear terms instead of being ambiguous. "So, it seems I will be doing this and this, while you're in charge of that and that..." is an excellent way to avoid future conflict from misunderstandings.

Relational Dynamics and Communication

'Relationships' is a broad term that covers a wide array of social connections. We've already established that we form a variety of relationships to meet our interpersonal needs. The stronger our relationships, the healthier we are— mentally and physically. This is why all relationships take work. Relationships take commitment and a willingness to learn and adapt.

The dynamics of our relationships depend on whether we're interacting with parents, partners, siblings, employer or employees, instructors, and friends, etc. We use different interpersonal communication methods depending on the kind of relationship we have with a person or a group of people. For instance, we'll be formal with employers and co-workers and casual with friends and siblings. We'll share some fears and secrets with partners and some with best friends. The methods we use and the kind of communication we employ are a reflection of the nature, importance, and effectiveness of that relationship to us.

Our expectations of a specific relationship depend on its nature and the needs or goals we want it to fulfill. For example, we will have different expectations from a parent, sibling, spouse, a doctor, and a co-worker. You can't expect your doctor to console you when you lose your job, can you? A friend better meets that need. For this reason, we use different rules to guide our behavior when we relate to each. You'd be hesitant to call your doctor or employer after business hours, whereas you'd reach out to a family member or friend regardless of how late it is.

We also measure the effectiveness of these relationships based on our criteria and goals for the particular relationship. Despite the differences that reflect on the kind of relationship we share with people, there are some commonalities in the way we approach or communicate during our interactions.

Relationships start, and then they end. This is an accepted truth. But what happens and why it happens is often a mystery to most of us. Knapp's relationship model demystifies this for us.

Knapp's Relationship Escalation Model

Coming together

I. Initiation

This stage is all about forming or setting impressions. In a social context, we'd be worrying about how we dress, how we speak, or how we present ourselves. Remember the effort you made on a first date? In a professional context, we'd be looking at amiability, shared goals, etc. Remember all the 'energy' or hustle-bustle at the office when a prospective client or business partner is expected. Regardless of the situation (personal or business), our objective is to 'catch attention' and be perceived as likable. Interaction at this stage is usually brief and ritualistic. Think handshakes, smiles, superficial conversation, etc.

II. Experimentation

Once we've created or shown an interest, we need to explore 'potential' and reduce uncertainty. This stage is also called the probing stage, as each side will analyze the other for a common interest. This stage is characterized by less formal and less superficial communication. Shared interests help further relationship goals. Remember that date that ended early because neither you nor the other person had anything to talk about? In a professional context, both parties will use the information they gather at this stage to decide if there's any mutual benefit in extending a business relationship.

III. Intensifying

The 'whirlwind' stage where relationships actually begin to take off. As both partners' comfort levels grow, they start revealing personal information they'd never dream of sharing with complete strangers. Activities are used to nurture relationships, and expectations increase. In a professional context, this is the stage where negotiations take place, and commitments are sought.

IV. Integration

By now, people's comfort levels with each other have grown by leaps and bounds, and they feel ready to increase the intimacy levels in their relationships. Plans are made, and serious commitments are discussed. Think shared bank accounts, apartment hunting so partners can live in one unit, getting a pet together, etc. In business relationships, both sides will begin to see "profit" or mutual financial benefits.

V. Bonding

In this stage, relationship status is shared with close friends, family members, and even the workplace. Relationship recognition is sought, and sometimes legal commitments follow. This bonding stage for business relationships grows to include partnerships. Greater profit is sought through exploration in areas such as lower business expenses for both sides.

Knapp's Relationship Termination Model

Coming apart

As relationships progress in a personal or professional context, misunderstandings occur, and conflicts arise. Eventually, these are either resolved or cause relationships to come apart.

I. Differentiating

In this stage, people in a relationship begin to think individually rather than with their partners. For instance, taking up different hobbies instead of pursuing the same hobby together. Distance grows between partners, and the early interest and partnership factors begin to fade. In business, external factors such as pressures, dealings with customers or dealers, etc., lead to a reduction in the number of meetings. Business partnerships also begin to look more like individual interests rather than mutual goals.

II. Circumscribing

Once differences crop up, partners will limit their conversations and set up boundaries. Feelings will not be discussed, and people find fewer topics or activities in common. Arguments or conflicts are avoided, and most people will insist on having their personal space and separate activities. Interaction becomes increasingly superficial. In a professional context, the communication gap deepens, issues regarding quality arise, and conflicts lead to a search for alternative partners.

III. Stagnation

As neither side has approached the other for fear of conflicts, or personal reasons like pride and ego, relationships begin to stagnate and decline further. Communication gaps become more glaring, and whatever limited interaction there is, is laden with strife. In business relationships, one or both sides will feel neglected or insignificant. There is usually no scope for improvement in relationships once they reach this stage.

IV. Avoidance

In a social context, partners feel physically detached. This growing distance, perceived or otherwise, forces them to avoid all forms of communication. On a business level, both sides avoid each other as the basis for their fundamental functioning has been irreversibly affected.

V. Terminating

The last stage of all relationships. In a social context, partners take different paths as unifying reasons (shared property, vested interests, children, etc.) can no longer keep them together. Similarly, business agreements end, and both sides go on to establish new agreements with other ventures.

Relationships are tricky. Most never move past the initial stages, and only some avoid ending up in the 'coming apart' stages. Some relationships jump or skip a few stages; it all depends on the partners (personal or business relationships) and how they deal with conflict, distance, and communication gaps. The more we learn about relationships, how they work, what causes conflicts, and how to negotiate and resolve disputes, the better our chances of establishing healthier and longer-lasting relationships.

Chapter 6: Important Communication Barriers/Mistakes/Obstacles

Communication is not just the simple act of sending a message. Several factors come into play after a message has been sent that determines the communication's success or failure. These can range from the sender's medium to delivery to the recipient's listening and decoding process, etc. The potential for communication to be distorted is present at all stages.

Both the sender and receiver must understand the communication process, barriers, and fixes to ensure that the communication is effective.

Common Barriers

Jargon

Which of us doesn't love a good TV series? The fast-paced life of doctors, the driven-for-justice cop or detective, the narcissistic but effective lawyer, and so on. Even during our favorite series, we will come across certain episodes where we find ourselves confused and lost. The slew of highly technical terms and explanations that screenwriters employ to draw on credibility makes messages abstract and confusing for people. It prevents them from understanding important information.

Often in our lives, we speak to one another in technical language or jargon as well. We find this efficient. However, most times, we don't realize that the person we're speaking with has little or no professional exposure to our industry. For example, a junior employee at the office would have no idea what P&L stands for, and someone from a non-marketing or sales division would not understand what the term KPI means. Equally, a homemaker with no professional experience at all would probably not understand any of this either.

When interacting with others, be it in a social or professional context, we must remember to be mindful of their listening comfort levels and their professional background to ensure that our message is received in the way that we intended. In making this effort, our conversational partners will feel more involved. By keeping things simple, they'll also participate in the conversation productively.

Emotional Barriers and Taboos

Ever seen Facebook (or another social media platform) light up with comments, genuine and from trollers, the second someone posts something political or religious?

In your childhood, you must have heard adults set rules like "Don't talk politics at the dinner table."

People have values and belief systems. They tend to defend these passionately. Trying to convince someone you know of something different is hard. Doing so with strangers using a written medium that has one of the highest chances of being misinterpreted is bound to earn you an emotion-filled response. This is perhaps why most of us establish limits regarding what topics can or can't be discussed and where they should or shouldn't be discussed.

Consider this conversation.

>**Daughter:** But daddy, I just want to talk about...
>
>**Father:** No, there will be no such discussion under my roof!
>
>**Daughter:** Please, daddy...
>
>**Father:** I said no, and that's all there is to be said.

The emotions other people trigger in us (and vice versa) during a conversation and subjects that we consider taboo (political, religious, racism, unpopular opinions, etc.) are significant communication barriers.

Consider workplace situations that evoke mixed emotions—discussions regarding performance, promotions, annual appraisals, bonuses, etc. Recall the last meeting you were part of and whether you refrained from voicing your opinion, and why you felt as though you shouldn't contribute.

Think about the last few times you didn't confront your partner, spouse, parent, or child about something that you felt strongly about. What led you to avoid that discussion?

Fear, mistrust, and suspicion are common human emotions that create communication barriers. We often worry about being negatively judged if we speak up. The severity depends entirely on our cultural or familial background—an Asian would probably have more trouble discussing their needs or disagreeing with seniors (authority) than a Westerner, for instance.

Emotion flare-ups can happen so suddenly in the midst of a conversation that we do and say things contrary to what we should have. We don't have reflex control over how emotions affect our communication. But it is a type of control we need to develop. An acute understanding of words, situations, topics that trigger emotional reactions, and early preparation on how to handle these will diminish the effect of emotion on our communication.

Information Overload

We've all been in conversations where the other person says one thing five different ways. And after an hour of rambling, during which they didn't give you a minute to put in your two cents, you're left with excess information and no clue what to do with it.

Information overload is a common occurrence. It happens in our personal lives and professional careers. Remember that one-hour training session that went into painful levels of micro-detail?

There's no shortage of information that we can share when making a presentation, holding a team or client meeting, training a new employee, or explaining our product requirements to a shopkeeper or sales executive.

Sometimes, we lack confidence in how we communicate. And so, we add as much detail as possible, believing that it makes our message clearer. We often don't realize that information overload affects the audience and makes it challenging for them to understand the communication.

Conciseness and brevity are essential, as we should share only what is most relevant, i.e., the parts we want the audience to focus on.

Differences in Perception and Viewpoint

We're all familiar with phrases like "looking glass" and "rose-tinted glasses." It isn't the first time we're confronted with the fact that everyone sees the world differently. When people don't see situations, contexts, nonverbal cues, visual communication, etc., the same way, how can we ensure our communication's integrity? But this difference in perception and viewpoint is also the most powerful reason to improve our communication skills. After all, the better we communicate, the greater the likelihood that our message will be seen exactly as we intended.

Other Communication Barriers:

- Lack of attention and interest, presence of distractions, and degree of relevance (at the subject level) to the receiver

- Physical handicaps such as hearing impairments and speech difficulties

- Language differences and miscommunications from unfamiliar accents

- Expectations, conjecture, prejudices, assumptions, and stereotyping

- Personal agenda (when we listen for the sole purpose of formulating our next response and aren't fully attentive to the speaker's message)

- Mirroring other people's communication styles

- Gender differences (women speak more freely and are more prone to mixing logic and emotion, whereas men talk in a linear and logical way)

Communication Barriers We've Discussed Previously:

- **Psychological**

    Opinions, attitudes, emotions, biases, mood swings, etc.

- **Physiological**

    Ill health, general discomfort, temperature-related distractions, feelings like hunger or the need to go to the bathroom, etc.

- **Physical**

    Workspace design flaws, sending messages across spaces, for instance, from one room to another without physically crossing this space, technology-enabled communication, etc.

- **Systematic**

    Inefficient structure, hierarchy, communication channels, especially in the workplace

- Attitudinal

    Behavior-related noise such as personality conflicts

Organizational-Level Communication Barriers

Communication barriers don't just occur in our personal lives or interpersonal interaction. In fact, there are more significant communication barriers in the workplace, and the challenges to effective communication are more evident than anywhere else. Look around your office, and you'll find people of all ages. This is typically referred to as a multigenerational workplace. Interaction with people from different generations, the rise of work from home employees, a globally placed workforce, and the use of new, constantly changing communication technology all present potential to cause misunderstandings and misinterpretations. Let's examine some of these in detail.

1. Communication Styles

Everyone has a different communication method, and these differences in communication styles and skills can create barriers between the sender and the receiver. Demography and culture, in particular, contribute to these different styles.

Think of the boss whose briefs are excruciatingly lengthy and the supervisor who only says a few words. The passionate, expressive speaker and the person whose tone is so neutral you can never tell if they're satisfied or not. The colleague who gestures a lot versus someone who refuses to speak but glares or uses other nonverbal communication forms. Learning to navigate through these confusing, contradictory, and often misleading communication styles can be challenging. To avoid creating additional barriers, we must remember to be confident, illustrate points with examples, remember to be brief, and ask for feedback from our audience to gauge their understanding levels.

2. Distance Related Barriers

With the changing business climate, more and more people either work from remote locations or home. Many companies depend on digital communication. These communication channels are not without their complications—from being unable to deduce nonverbal cues in emails to lack of rapid response to texts, rising frustration and anxiety from internet-related issues during conferences and meetings, to overcoming time zone limitations. Such physical barriers are even more evident when we consider blue-collar employees that have to manage without a designated working space. Over time, these challenges damage an organization, especially if they haven't figured out how best to leverage technology. Another issue that crops up when we examine remote work and tech-enabled communication is that of disengagement. The struggle to onboard several displaced teams, drive a culture of collaboration, and catch employee attention over oceans and the internet is all too real.

3. Organizational Structure

There are almost a dozen different management styles, several types of organization hierarchies, and half a dozen various organization structure types. The more complex and rigid the hierarchy or organizational structure, the more inefficient the organization's communication process.

4. Lack of Trust

Power, politics, shifting dynamics between senior team members, and the never-ending drama in organizations all lead to an environment where there is no trust. And when employees don't feel comfortable speaking up and have a general but widespread mistrust toward their leaders or managers, it affects the quality of communication.

Another aspect that affects trust within an organization is the lack of consistent communication channels. Every time an employee misses an update or important communication, it reduces employee engagement opportunities, increases suspicion and confusion, and directly impacts productivity.

5. Listening

Feedback and criticism aren't just a mid- or senior-level employee's prerogative. Even junior employees should be allowed to share their opinions and add value to their work environment. However, while most mid- to senior-level employees might have the experience to handle feedback and criticism with some degree of tact, junior employees don't. While this is not a reason not to allow them to contribute, organizations need to learn to sort through the noise. Equally, organizations that follow open workplace communication culture have a happier and more engaged workforce.

6. Finding that Balance

A new client has been onboarded, and a new project has popped up. Emails and messages are flying around the entire office. Important things go in the trash folder, irrelevant messages spam our inbox, and we find that half a day has gone into sifting through all this communication. An ignore-this-block-that policy ensues, and all critical future communication from the same sources is lost. A balance needs to be maintained (content localization) to keep communication channels open and free of messages irrelevant to different employees.

To establish that we are clear communicators at the workplace requires a lot more thought, effort, and patience as compared to social or interpersonal communication.

Developing empathy and being mindful of others can be beneficial as our endeavors will only serve to increase the quality of communication.

Overcoming Barriers

A skilled communicator can easily overcome most of the barriers mentioned above. Three essential skills that will help you bridge communication barriers are active listening, simplicity, and constructive feedback.

- **Active Listening**

    o Concentrating on the communication rather than just hearing the message is what differentiates regular communicators from skilled communicators. Active listening means listening in a way that improves mutual understanding. It not only makes us better communicators, but it also helps us solve problems. Using active listening in our daily lives has tremendous benefits, ranging from making our conversation partner feel heard to evoking positive emotions.

- **Simplicity**

    o Communication that is complex or filled with jargon has the potential to cause misunderstandings. It also distracts the listener and leaves others confused. It is thus vital to understand your target audience before speaking. Lengthy communication is unhelpful as well, as your listener might switch off, get distracted, and miss your message completely.

- **Constructive Feedback**
    - Feedback in communication means the signals or responses a sender receives that help them determine whether their communication was received as intended or whether it needs modifications. Like communication, feedback comes in many forms—verbal and nonverbal. Feedback is an essential communication tool that helps both the sender and receiver.

While barriers can never be eliminated, there are ways to reduce negative consequences and streamline communication. Understanding the causes of communication barriers and people's communication preferences is the first step toward effective communication.

Basic Communication Fixes

We communicate every day. Sometimes with one person, but more often our audience comprises many individuals. Every person we interact with has a different background and a preferred communication style. Preventing a communication breakdown starts with acknowledging these differences and understanding the consequences of communication barriers, such as lost trust.

What Leads to Communication Breakdowns?

Should we blame a failure in communication on employees or systemic issues in company policies and culture? Perhaps a breakdown in communication happens over simple misunderstandings that escalate into something more.

Let's look at some of the more common reasons behind communication breakdowns.

- Ambiguously defined communication standards

- Selection of the means of communication (when to use email versus the efficiency of a quick phone call)

- Cultural differences and differences in communication styles

- Mixed messages

- Passive listening skills
- Too much or too little detail
- Conjecture, assumptions, or unresolved issues
- Lack of feedback, clarifying questions, or follow-through
- Personality clashes, conflicts, and general attitudinal negativity

One of the simplest ways to avoid a communication breakdown is to adopt healthy communication habits.

Pauses are Important

We've all heard the adage, "think before you speak." What was the explanation given along with this advice? For most of us, the adage reminds us that we shouldn't speak on impulse. We're told that impulsive communication can leave us with regrets. But what are some of the other advantages to pauses?

Pausing before you reply to communication can help you avoid common communication pitfalls and accomplish three goals.

- You avoid interrupting the speaker

- You show the speaker that you have carefully considered their message

- By taking a moment to process what was said, you avoid the risk of jumping to conclusions

Clarifications

Assuming that we have understood what the other person is saying is a poor communication habit. Even when we listen actively, we're bound to have missed something, and in the absence of complete details, we use conjecture. Instead of handling doubt ourselves, ask the speaker to clarify. A simple question like, "could you explain that please?" or "what do you mean?" followed by a pause works wonderfully.

The speaker will then add further explanations or provide extensive answers—all of which will help build your understanding of the communication.

Paraphrase

Don't be afraid or hesitant to add nonverbal cues. Something as simple as a nod or a smile can encourage the speaker and give them the signals they need to gauge their communication effectiveness. Before responding, you can say, "Let me see if I got that right..." or, "What you're trying to say is..." And then repeat the message in your words as you have understood it.

Not only do you show that you've genuinely paid attention, but you also demonstrate that you've made every effort to understand. If there is a misunderstanding, the speaker will then correct it before it causes any complications.

Listen More and Talk Less

The human brain can process information at lightning speed. However, as soon as we begin to run several functions simultaneously, our focus shifts, and we miss a few things. Refraining from speaking while the sender is talking will help us to hear them better. Listening also builds trust. When people feel heard and valued, they trust you more.

The 3-Second Look

When you're dealing with someone you suspect isn't telling the truth, instead of continuing the conversation, pause and look at them. Not an uncomfortable glare. Just a typical curious stare. People tend to stumble when they lie if pressured to explain themselves. You'll eventually get the truth and more details—all of which will prevent you from jumping to conclusions or acting on misinformation.

How to Avoid and Fix Communication Breakdowns Within a Team

1. Be Human

Remember that the members of your team are people. They aren't cogs in a machine. They aren't robots that will work tirelessly. They have needs. They make mistakes. They need to learn and grow. Appreciation costs you nothing, but it means the world to your team. Build a culture that fosters trust and loyalty and empowers your team members.

2. Connect Departments and Employees

While your team is loyal to you and perhaps even your department, what happens when something wasn't delivered as expected? Who is blamed? "The other department didn't do what they were supposed to." Isn't that a standard explanation? People don't feel comfortable shifting the spotlight to colleagues they have to work with every day, let alone colleagues they have a strong interpersonal relationship with. And so, the blame is shifted to a nameless, faceless person in another department. Foster cohesiveness between all departments by increasing visibility. Feature people on the company's intranet, internal sites, publications, etc. Don't encourage departments to work in silos. Why? Because sometimes, what seems like a communication breakdown is a relationship issue.

3. Use Quick and Convenient Communication Channels

Now that the world is seeing a shift toward greater need for and dependency on virtual communication, it is prudent to help teams communicate through a common, readily available virtual platform. While you're exploring options, consider project management tools as well. They enable teams to stay organized and make it easier for people to track progress. When teams remain on schedule, it reduces the likelihood of miscommunication.

4. Don't Be Afraid to Check-in

Micromanagement can happen all too easily. Even when it is not intended. However, misinterpretations or a lack of understanding can derail a project. Checking in with teams to gauge their understanding, monitoring a project's progress, and touching base with key stakeholders can make a big difference.

5. Embrace and Encourage Feedback and Questions

Fear, mistrust, and suspicion are emotions commonly seen in a rigid workplace. When a work environment is fraught with negative emotions, people are hesitant to communicate. Most people are constantly on the defensive and feel as though they cannot be completely honest with each other. For instance, junior members can become afraid of asking questions as they feel experienced members will shame them for not understanding their task. By encouraging questions and enforcing a genuine feedback process, communication breakdowns can be minimized. Feedback will also allow senior members to identify potential issues and address them.

Communication breakdowns aren't a mild annoyance. They have serious financial implications as businesses can lose huge deals. Communication breakdowns also cause friction between employees, management, and departments. Productivity levels fall dramatically. Ambiguity in communication also increases human error as employees misunderstand their goals, responsibilities, business processes, and company policies.

Communication breakdowns are incredibly expensive, and good communication practices need to be encouraged and enforced from the top down to ensure a business's success.

Chapter 7 Part 1: Improving Communication Skills

Communication in its varied forms developed because humans needed to pass information between themselves. Sometimes the information being shared was simple enough to use nonverbal cues—shake of a head as a warning or disapproval, a smile as a gesture of encouragement or approval, for instance. Often, information was so complex that it needed to be shared with visual or verbal methods. As the complexity levels of our information sharing grew, so did our ability to communicate.

Communication is crucial to our survival and the development of our communities and relationships. Without communication, we would have no connections. We would have no society. As social animals, how we connect with one another defines us. Communication also aids in the development of our perception of ourselves. Communicating with others freely can help us reinforce positive beliefs and reduce influences on negative thought patterns. The ability to communicate is directly linked to both our physical and mental well-being.

Communication is core to all interactions including how we work with others and the smooth functioning of our teams.

How we communicate ideas and how we receive them furthers our learning and growth as people and professionals. Strengthening communication skills will thus allow us to enjoy greater success in every area of our lives.

Top Communication Skills

Communication skills, or soft skills, develop every time we interact with other people. The enhanced ability to share our thoughts, ideas, emotions, etc., can help us get ahead in our lives and at the workplace.

Let's look at some of the top communication skills that enable us to lead a more fulfilled life.

- Emotional intelligence
- Clarity
- Empathy
- Confidence
- Listening
- Keeping an open mind

Emotional Intelligence (EI)

EI helps us to modulate and regulate our emotional response. Communication and information sharing can often evoke deep emotions. Emotions aren't always positive and can often influence us to act in undesirable ways. Developing high EI means we'll be less reactionary. We're better communicators when our messages are not distorted with emotional undertones.

Clarity

Consider this narrative:

Just as I left home this morning, it started to rain. I missed my first university class. But then met up with a friend. By the time I returned late at night, I was still warm and dry. My friend and I spent the evening playing games. My mother asked me to drop off her mail when I went home to fetch an umbrella. Lunch was a shabby affair.

Clarity and cohesion, even chronology, are not quite right in this narrative. Learning to formulate thoughts, ensuring proper sequence progression in messages, and being clear about what it is that we want to communicate checks misunderstandings and misinterpretations.

Empathy

Empathy is our ability to connect with another person on an emotional level. We become better communicators when we can relate to others' feelings.

Confidence

Confidence comes with belief. If you believe your message, you'll convey it more confidently. If you're confident of your abilities, you'll project competence. And competence and confidence inspire trust. When people hear a confident speaker, they will be more receptive to the communication.

Listening

Since listening is an integral part of communication, we cannot grow into competent communicators without working on our listening abilities. Without proper listening skills, we will not receive messages as they were intended, nor will we be able to contribute to a dialogue.

Open-mindedness

Being receptive to others' ideas and flexible in our approach to new information is essential to our continued growth. It is also a skill that we depend on when we interact with culturally diverse teams. Most times, flexibility and open-mindedness are confused with indecision. However, by challenging our beliefs and welcoming new experiences, by being flexible and adapting to the needs of the situation, we become better communicators.

A Little Thinking Exercise:

- Think about the one person you found yourself gravitating toward as soon as they started to speak. What is it about that person that grabbed your attention with their first word? Were they able to influence you or persuade you effortlessly?

- Do you frown and turn away from others the minute they start to talk? What is it about that person or their words that made you react that way?

- When people talk about being persuasive, what does it mean to you? Do you often hear advice like "engage your audience" when you're preparing for a presentation or a speech? Why is engaging your audience so important?

- Think about the most entertaining or boring wedding toast or work-related presentation you've attended. What were the qualities of the speakers that you admired or didn't approve of?

What is Persuasion?

Persuasion is the art of changing someone's mind or behavior. We are successful persuaders when we can influence a person to do or believe something different from what they initially believed.

Consider this scenario: You've never liked the color orange. And yet when you last went shopping with a friend, they were able to convince you to try an orange dress or a shirt.

What was it they said, or how did they say it, that persuaded you to try that article of clothing?

How Does it Increase Our Communication Effectiveness?

In its simplest form, communication is the sending and receiving of messages, while persuasion is convincing someone to put aside their beliefs and values and accept yours. You can't have one without the other.

In a social context: Almost every interpersonal interaction is a persuasion attempt—let's not watch this movie, how about we eat that for dinner, why don't we do this weekend activity, we should pick this school not that because... Even something as simple as "hey, listen to me."

In a professional context: No matter what role or industry you work in, your effectiveness is determined by your ability to influence and inspire action. Hierarchy not in consideration, anyone in any business who needs someone else to stop and listen, accept, and act on the sender's message is employing persuasive skills. Every pitch, presentation, negotiation, and conversation will require you to have effective persuasion abilities. Persuasion is an important tool when it comes to conflict resolution as well.

Since persuasion and communication work in tandem, persuasion becomes a key element in your efforts to become an effective communicator, especially in the workplace. Persuasion is an important but challenging skill to develop. People have values and beliefs that they defend passionately. Depending on their background and experiences, they would have formed a unique understanding of how the world operates. These become their "truths," and any attempt to change or challenge a person's truth will make them resistant. Take discussions about gun control or campaigns to switch to a vegetarian diet, as examples. How do people respond when ideas and beliefs they aligned themselves with are challenged?

To be a persuasive influencer, you must have the skills to influence, motivate people to accept your ideas, and act on them. These skills are crucial to reinforce your image as a future-thinking, global leader. You also must be influenceable. What does this entail? To consider different options open-mindedly, actively listen to different sides of an argument, and weigh different opinions without prejudice or bias and then make decisions.

Communications are of different kinds. Sometimes you may simply want to inform the listeners of something new.

The purpose of this kind of communication is to share knowledge. Your goal is to ensure that your audience has fully understood this knowledge. For instance, a workshop on digitalization transformation will seek to impart knowledge or inform the listeners.

Then there's persuasion. The objective here is to get the listeners to perform an action based on the knowledge shared. So, if we change direction during the workshop and start to pitch the benefits of digitalization, we're employing persuasive communication. Our goal then would be to convince them to try digitalization in areas where they haven't already. We're considered successful if our idea is accepted and the organization explores how to leverage the power of digitalization.

To be persuasive, you must understand what motivates your audience. This means gauging what is important to them. Audience analysis then becomes a key skill. The more you understand your audience's motivation, the more effective your communication. On the other hand, if you fail, your presentation will not have the desired impact. Having an audience-centered approach also means being able to anticipate how they might react to your communication.

If listeners like what they are hearing, they begin to generate positive thoughts which result in the acceptance of your message. Your message is likely to be rejected if your listeners dislike what they're hearing, as your attempt would have generated negative thoughts. This generation of these thoughts is called elaboration. The more involved your audience, the greater the chances that they will elaborate on it. Persuasion is thus an active process.

What are the Signs of Acceptance?

Here is where your ability to read nonverbal cues and analyze verbal communication come into play. When people are accepting of your suggestions, they will respond with positive affirmation. This could be in the form of "how" and "what" questions. For instance, "how do we do this" or "what can we do next?" You'll see the ideal body language for such a situation, such as leaning forward, eagerness in facial expressions, even clapping or smiling. When your audience remains unconvinced, you're more likely to hear "why" questions. Finally, the most accurate way of gauging persuasion is to ask for feedback.

Chapter 7 Part 2: How to Talk to Anyone

Everyone has a different way of communicating. We can separate people into four categories based on their communication style—hostile, indifferent, uninformed, and supportive. You've most likely already interacted with people who fit into each of these categories. You've applied your communication style and techniques during your interaction. What was the result? A growing sense of frustration each time you fail to be convincing?

Learning about these communication styles, identifying which category people you interact with fit into, and applying style-specific communication strategies will significantly impact your communication effectiveness.

Communication Styles

When we talk about communication both in the context of in-person interaction and virtual communication, we're essentially faced with one common issue—the changing nature of how we communicate.

Attention spans are not what they used to be. Everyone's focus is everywhere. Catching someone's attention, getting them to listen to us, and shrinking our message to communicate in a much shorter time are some of the challenges that we face.

If we want to convince, if we want to inform, if we want to negotiate or persuade, we have to think about what we're saying and how we're saying it. This means we have to know our listener's communication style and their motivations to be effective.

The Four Communication Styles:

#1 Hostile

A person with a hostile communication style is verbally aggressive. Think of the person who has no qualms disagreeing with you openly. The loud person who is known to be vocal about their opinions, specifically the negative ones e.g. I don't like this. I don't agree with that. This is not going to work.

This kind of communication style typically lends itself to certain professions like engineers and accountants. The technically minded person in your team who is great to have around but who requires logic-based and direct communication.

How do you communicate with people with a hostile communication style? How do you persuade them?

The first thing to remember is that they are not physically aggressive. They are called hostile communicators because they are quite blunt and direct. They come off as intimidating because their communication counterpart(s) will always be anxious about being openly disagreed with and interrupted.

What makes people hostile communicators?

People who fit into this category instinctively put the information they receive into categories. When communication doesn't fit into one of their categories, they cannot process it. It leaves them feeling annoyed or impatient. To communicate with such a person means categorizing information for them. Whether in verbal or written, or visual form, information must be concise and separated into categories, bullet points, and more categories.

Consider the following email example:

> Good morning Lou,
>
> I need your help with the following things.
>
> 1. Can you edit my presentation slides before Tuesday?
>
> 2. Schedule a team conference for the following Thursday.

3. Let me know when you're free to discuss the pre-meeting agenda.

By ensuring that our message is easy for a hostile communicator to process, we earn their cooperation.

#2 Indifferent

As the name suggests, people who fit into this communication style category are typically the ones who lack enthusiasm and the impulse to act on information. Even when you're speaking with them, their impassivity is evident in their tone and facial expression. Think of the person who nods along and is prone to saying, "Yes, yes, sure. Okay," but then not taking action like you'd expect them to.

This kind of communication style typically lends itself to people who have been in an administrative or bureaucratic position for a long time. They have a very specific job and feel uncomfortable being asked to do anything outside of it. Deviating from tasks is not something you'll see them doing.

How do you communicate with people with an indifferent communication style? How do you persuade them?

The first thing to remember is that indifferent communicators will never commit to anything.

Consider the following exchange:

> **Person A:** Do you think you could look over my presentation slides by Tuesday?
>
> **The indifferent communicator:** Perhaps. I'm not sure. Leave it on my desk or send it by email, and I'll get around to it when I have some time.

What makes people indifferent communicators?

Most people adopt an indifferent communication style when they feel unfulfilled and unimportant. Think of the person who goes to the office every day, files papers, and then returns home. Where is the excitement in their role? What sense of purpose do they find in their careers? Which part of their position would make them feel needed and important? Like clogs in a machine, they function as they're supposed to, and they are unwilling to do much else.

Making communication effective and prompting indifferent communicators into action mode is as simple as instilling a sense of importance. How do you do that? By asking for help and advice.

Let's go back to our earlier example and see what it should look like to be effective with an indifferent communicator.

> **Person A:** Do you have a minute? I could really use your help with something.

The indifferent communicator: Perhaps. I'm not sure. Tell me what you need, and I'll think about it.

Person A: I have this presentation coming up, and I'm so confused about what content to use. I have narrowed it down to Option A and B. But I need someone who is an expert in this subject to give it a once over.

The indifferent communicator: That sounds like a lot of work. I don't know. Maybe.

Person A: My deadline is still a while away. If not today, let me know what day works for you. I could really use your help and would appreciate any time you can give me.

The indifferent communicator: How about tomorrow?

#3 Uninformed

As the name suggests, people who fit into this communication style category are typically the ones who aren't quite where you need them to be (information-wise, of course).

Consider the following exchange:

Person A: Could we speak about that post-meeting documentation I sent over earlier this week?

The uninformed communicator: Perhaps. I had glimpsed through it earlier, but I feel like I might have missed something. Can I go through it and get back to you?

This kind of communication style typically lends itself to people who are in a decision-making role or position. Everything you've been working toward rests on their approval or disapproval, and you can't seem to get them to act.

How do you communicate with people with an uninformed communication style? How do you persuade them?

The first thing to remember is that uninformed communicators need to feel understood—not their communication, but their situation. You've probably met enough people who fit into this category—the person who keeps saying they're busy or that they need more time or that they feel overwhelmed.

To connect with an uninformed communicator and to prompt them into action requires a two-part approach. You have to be empathetic. And go a step further by also asking them for their point of view.

Consider the exchange from before:

> **Person A:** Do you think you could look over my presentation slides by Tuesday?
>
> **The uninformed communicator:** I'm not sure. I've recently received several tasks, and they all need my attention. I'm feeling overwhelmed, and I don't know when I'll have time to look over the presentation slides.

How do you apply the Empathy and Point of View communication strategy with an uninformed communicator?

> **Person A:** Do you think you could look over my presentation slides?
>
> **The uninformed communicator**: I'm not sure. I've recently received several tasks, and they all need my attention. I'm feeling overwhelmed, and I don't know when I'll have time to look over the presentation slides.
>
> **Person A:** Hey, I know it's crazy at your end. I heard about all the things that were sent to you to be completed. But I really need your opinion on this. Do you think you can get to the slides by sometime next week?

The uninformed communicator: Next week might be more practical.

Person A: I'm so relieved. Thank you for taking some time for me. I know you're super busy, but can we speak on Tuesday?

The uninformed communicator: Maybe, I'm not sure. Tuesday is jam packed with meetings.

Person A: That's terrible. If the morning is not suitable, then how about late afternoon on Tuesday? I would really appreciate it.

The uninformed communicator: Sure, okay.

#4 Supportive

You can identify a supportive communicator by their constant need to be liked and recognized. This is the kind of person who says yes to everything. They are the kind of person who is always trying to organize and create cohesiveness in a team. Let's have a get-together. How about a team meeting? I think that idea is just fantastic. We should totally do that.

However, when you need them to commit, you'll rarely find a satisfactory response.

This kind of communication style typically lends itself to people who have an unshakeable need to be liked by everyone. They are constantly consumed by thoughts of how people will react to them or their actions.

How do you communicate with people with an uninformed communication style? How do you persuade them?

The main thing to remember is that communication and persuasion become significantly more effective if you feed their need for approval. To open a communication channel with a supportive communicator, it isn't enough to say something as simple as "good morning" or "hello." Even small chit-chat like "how was the weekend?" will only earn you a one or two-word answer like "fine" or "great."

The best approach is ask-and-reveal.

Here's an example:

> Morning! How was the weekend? Mine was so busy. I kept meaning to fix the driveway but never got around to it. What did you do?

That's the kind of ask-and-reveal communication that will instantly win over the supportive communicator. Since they tend to relate to people they feel are "like them," you'll have created an immediate bond by drawing on similarities. Now that you have your foot in the door, it's time to get to the business end of the conversation. It is imperative to remember that the supportive communicator's need to be liked is what makes them pliable.

Continued conversation:

> **Person A**: Morning! How was the weekend? Mine was so busy. I kept meaning to fix the driveway but never got around to it. What did you do?
>
> **Supportive communicator:** I know, right? Where does time fly when you're on leave? I was supposed to mow the lawn but just didn't get to it.
>
> **Person A**: I hear ya, buddy. Listen, I need some help. I've spoken to almost everyone in this department, and they've all said that you're the best person to help me out.
>
> **Supportive communicator:** Wow. I didn't know that. But yes, what do you need?
>
> **Person A**: Can you edit these presentation slides for me?
>
> **Supportive communicator:** I don't know. I'm super busy right now.

Person A: I know! Everyone says you're doing the work of the whole team! Where would we be without you?

Supportive communicator: I'm flattered. Do you think these can wait until next week?

Person A: Sure. Does Monday work for you?

Supportive communicator: Not quite. How about Tuesday?

Person A: Sure, and if you finish by lunch, we can have coffee together! I'm buying.

Understanding and Leveraging Motivations

Consider this scenario: You are in charge of a team at the office, and you need to motivate them to deliver a project. While everyone else has understood their tasks and are busy working toward their deadline, one team member doesn't seem to be carrying their weight. What do you do? How do you spur them into action? You've exhausted yourself trying to talk to them. You've explained in bullet points or employed empathy and point of view and other strategies. And you are yet to see results.

Oftentimes, merely interacting with people based on their communication style is not enough to motivate or persuade them. It isn't enough to grab their attention and make them listen. In such cases, it benefits to have another tool—one that helps you to understand the person's (one or several) motivations in that specific moment of communication. By identifying and addressing these motivations, your communication efforts will receive a tremendous boost. Loop in the tips on persuasion abilities, and you cannot go wrong.

The Three Main Underlying Motivations

#1 Achievement

While achieving goals in a team setting or via a team effort is a wonderful thing—we are social creatures, after all—sometimes people just want individual recognition. Being recognized for what they've achieved on their own via their own merit can be genuinely motivating to them. Oftentimes, it can be a more powerful influencer than money and position.

Identifying an achievement-based person: You're looking for a loner—a person who is always alone at their workstation. An achievement-based person is continually working. They work all sorts of extra hours. You'll also find that an achievement-based person is always on the go. Their constant thought is, I just have to get this done. Another way to identify an achievement-based person is by their need for feedback. Since feedback is the means to better performance, they're aching for some input.

Characteristics: An achievement-driven person is open to taking moderate risks. They understand that there is no reward without risk. They are open to trying new things because they want to achieve.

Communication strategies: An achievement-based person needs to be put on a stricter timeline than other people. They need to feel as though their task is insurmountable. Without that additional pressure, there can be no distinguishing, recognizable achievement. After all, if anyone can do it, why does accomplishing that task make them unique? Assigning a task in front of other team members will prove more fruitful than giving them a slightly unreasonable goal. By entrusting them with something meaningful and risky, you underscore your faith and belief in them. By implying that they're a crucial cog in the team, you're giving them the chance to make an impact with their task achievement. And with the challenge you present to them, you open doors to the possibility of being recognized for an achievement.

> **Example**: Our target for this quarter needs to be achieved in three weeks. Lou, do you think you can do it in two? Less perhaps? What do you think?

#2 Affiliation

Like a supportive communicator, an affiliation-motivated person is just looking to get along with a group. They are motivated by others' opinions about them and their actions, and they are obsessed with maintaining harmony. Their motivation to be affiliated to anything, a group or project, is to gain acceptance.

Identifying an affiliation-based person: An affiliation-motivated person is always trying to talk to several people at once. They love the concept of an open working environment. The need to belong to a group, to feel like an integral part of it, leads them to constantly organize an activity. Their need to be liked also supersedes their need to get things done.

Characteristics: An affiliation-motivated person avoids risk. They don't like rocking the boat or causing friction as it will disturb the group's harmony. If you want to do something risky, an affiliation-motivated person will be supportive. However, they'll caution you at every step.

Communication strategies: To influence and interact with an affiliation-motivated person, you need to approach every situation as though it's going to disrupt the group. Take, for example, a request to a manager for new hardware or software for the team. Simply filling out forms or sending out emails is insufficient to communicate the "need" for such a significant expense. Hinging the entire teams' performance and state of harmony on the new software or hardware will, however, influence them to make concessions.

#3 Power

Power or influence is the more misunderstood of the three underlying motivations. People who fit into this category have an acute understanding that only by building influence can they get things done.

Identifying an influence-based person: A power-motivated person has a desperate need to be involved with everything. They'll get upset if they haven't been included in every conference, email, or communication. They want to be the decision-makers, and they want to win every argument.

Characteristics: A power-motivated person is institution or organization minded. They build power and influence in an organization and within their teams and then use this to motivate their colleagues and subordinates to be more productive. A power-motivated person also has a high need to implement all sorts of efficient practices to reduce their work. This makes them great at delegating.

Communication strategies: Communicating with a power-motivated person, most likely your manager since it's improbable they'll be at a junior position, requires tact. How do you do it? Asking for advice, patronage, and help are your go-to strategies as it allows them to feel as though they have influence.

Consider this example: You're in charge of growing sales in your region. When you develop a plan and share it with your power-motivated boss, they're highly likely to either disapprove, micromanage, or change everything. Get them involved in the decision-making process. Share with them that you have outlined two or three alternatives and that you'd love their input or feedback on which of the options would work best.

Developing Social Intelligence

Our ability to communicate and form relationships, learning from failures in social settings, and interacting with people using tact or "street smarts" is termed Social Intelligence (SI). It is also commonly referred to as Social Quotient (SQ).

While Emotional Intelligence (EI) or Emotional Quotient (EQ) refers to our ability to perceive emotions and manage them, SI/SQ is about interpersonal skills and people's behavior toward each other.

People with high SI/SQ typically have the following traits:

- They can start and maintain conversations with people from all walks of life, using appropriate language, tone, and tact.

- They're adept at switching between different social roles.

- They have excellent listening skills as they go beyond merely hearing and interpreting verbal communication.

- They are quick to identify a person's motivation by merely listening to them and observing their behavior.

- Personality clashes are rare with a SI/SQ high individual.

- They are conscious of how they portray themselves to others. This is a hard skill to master as it requires a balance between image management control and being authentic.

Social intelligence helps us figure out the best way to get along with others. It helps guide us when we are faced with difficult situations. Favorable outcomes are not possible without SI/SQ. Even if you are the best at sports or academics or work, all your relationships will suffer without adequate SI/SQ skills. As a result, you'll lose out on personal and professional opportunities.

Examples of situations where we employ our SI/SQ skills include distinguishing between the right time to switch between speaking and listening and knowing what to say and what to do. Learning to time when we should speak and what we should say at that moment is a critical part of social intelligence—for instance, using humor to comfort a friend who has recently lost a family member. Your intentions are good—you wanted to lift your friend's spirit. But the timing is very wrong, and you'll come off as insensitive, aloof, and lacking in sympathy and empathy.

Social intelligence, like communication skills, develops as we mature. We observe others and learn. We find ourselves in a sticky situation and learn to navigate it till we reach a favorable outcome. SI/SQ abilities are essential if we want to become effective communicators. In a professional context, SI/SQ abilities help promote teamwork and create a productive work environment.

Until recently, teaching SI/SQ abilities was not a priority. This is because people automatically pick up SI/SQ skills. However, in recent years, the emphasis on learning and acquiring social intelligence has increased as it is an indispensable skill. Not only is it a significant contributor to good work cultures, having strong SI/SQ abilities will ensure employment in an era of increasing automation.

Lack of exposure and understanding of cultural differences are barriers to effective communication. Research has shown that SI/SQ development can lead to positive intercultural interactions. Ours is a globalized workplace, and interaction with other cultures is unavoidable. By strengthening our SI/SQ abilities, we can facilitate intercultural communication and collaboration at the workplace.

How Can We Develop Social Intelligence?

Like anything else in life, some people are naturally gifted when it comes to SI/SQ abilities. However, for most of us, we must work to develop these skills.

Here are some steps that we can take to boost our SI/SQ skills.

Being mindful and observant of other people. Many of our actions are automatic when we interact with other people. We often multitask so instinctively that we don't realize that we're not in a position to catch nonverbal cues. How many times have we spoken to others without lifting our gaze from our phone or laptop screens? If we want to pick up on what people are feeling or on the emotions they are expressing, we need to make an active effort to observe their social cues. Go a step forward and use all other senses to decode, read between the lines, identify deception, and to push till we get to the core of the sender's state of emotion.

Enhance your emotional intelligence. EI/EQ is about understanding what others are feeling and experiencing. Without understanding what triggers certain behaviors, thoughts, and actions, how do you empathize with others? To know is to understand. There can be no tact, no human relationships, and no control over emotions in a social setting without SI.

What are some of the other tools that we can employ to improve our communication efforts?

Audience Analysis

We've all been in socially awkward situations. Remember when you told a joke or heard someone else tell a joke, and no one laughed? Perhaps someone got offended and stormed off and left everyone wondering what went wrong.

When we're in our social groups, we're aware of each person's background, experiences, beliefs, and values. We're careful about what we say so that we don't embarrass ourselves and upset others. However, when we're in an unfamiliar setting or amidst a group of people we only know superficially (think office meeting or virtual team conference), we need to understand our audience.

Audience analysis is the gathering of information about the people around us. By understanding the people we're with, by gauging their needs and expectations, by acknowledging their values and beliefs, we're better positioned to avoid alienating them.

Audience-Centered Approach to Communication

We've discussed how bias, prejudice, personality clashes, etc., are communication barriers. But how and why do such biases and prejudices come up? Why do personalities clash? How do you continue to communicate and work with people you can't always tolerate or like?

Don't Take It Personally.

Consider the following scenario:

> You are talking to someone, and they hurriedly get up and leave. It is rude to walk away when someone is speaking with you, is it not? And so, your first instinct is to attach meaning to that behavior. And in this scenario, a positive meaning is improbable. And so, you take it personally. After all, there is no opportunity to clarify, and it is instinctive to assume.

By taking things personally and jumping to conclusions, we develop annoyance and frustration, perhaps even a degree of distrust. The next time you interact with that person, those emotions will dominate and cause you to misinterpret that person. Attitude and prejudice are barriers to effective communication. A guideline for responding in such a situation is to turn all those negative emotions into something positive consciously. Leverage clarifying questions and feedback mechanisms to understand what prompted that behavior and then extend understanding and empathy.

Build Credibility.

When we are blindsided by material needs, by negative emotions like envy and greed, or we find ourselves in crisis or stress-evoking overwhelming situations, our decision-making skills are affected. At our core, humans are not evil. But certain conditions make it difficult to distinguish right from wrong, and we make a decision or do something unethical. When such truths are discovered, the consequences are seen in the ruination of relationships (personal and professional) and loss of reputation. For instance, being insincere can cause people to question or doubt you, even when you're telling the truth. When people speak, one of the first things the listener does is gauge for credibility. It is only when we establish trust and credibility that our listeners are open to our communication. So before doing or saying anything, first ask yourself how that action or interaction will affect the people around you. If it's going to hurt them, look for an alternative.

Look Beyond Undesirable Behavior.

Specific motivations and needs guide people to behave the way that they do. Behavior becomes undesirable when needs and motivations are unmet. For instance, someone who worked extensively on a deliverable is in search of recognition for their efforts. When that recognition does not come, you'll find that they bemoan everyone else's competence at the workplace. It's not that they don't like their counterparts. They just want someone, anyone, to acknowledge that they did well. Instead of passing judgment, being critical, and "reacting" to undesirable behaviors, take a moment to consider what the person needs and tailor your communication accordingly.

Be Flexible and Adaptable.

Why do we gravitate toward some people and away from others? Why do people keep saying that shared interests and thinking alike help people make friends or build relationships?

Everyone has a different way of doing things and a different way of interacting. There is no right way or wrong way; our way or their way. Instead of looking at them and wondering why they do things a particular way, we should be flexible and adaptable in our communication and approach. In doing so, we make people feel safe and valued. We connect with people on a level that they're familiar with. And when we form that connection, people shift and start to mirror us.

Key Takeaways

Communication is the heart of everything that we do and all the relationships that we form and maintain. Most people struggle with poor connections, be it at work or on the personal front. The manager you can't seem to speak to, the new colleague you don't know how to strike up a conversation with, the friction at home over being unable to persuade a spouse or a partner over parenting techniques and what works and why, the friend who is always upset because of something you said, the parent who constantly bemoans how you never seem to listen— the battles we face because of barriers in communication are endless.

It is easy to feel hopeless and discouraged. What most people don't know is that with just a few fixes in their communication abilities and styles, the root cause of the friction they experience will settle.

As listeners, we can improve how we process incoming messages through steps such as learning to listen, decoding nonverbal cues, being aware of and managing emotions, using questions for clarification, and the feedback process.

Similarly, as speakers, we can be more conscious about how we transmit communication by using pauses or time to reflect on what we are about to say, weighing how it affects the person, whether it's ethical, and employing Social and Emotional Intelligence. Being wary of humor, treating people equally, putting away biases and prejudices to facilitate communication, being sensitive to cultural differences, and resolving conflicts before they mushroom into something bigger are proactive steps that we can consciously adopt to encourage people to respond to our communication positively.

Finally, we can incorporate audience analysis, the art of negotiation and persuasion, addressing the emotional and motivation needs of our listeners, and strategizing our communication based on the other person's communication style to support our endeavors.

Above all, we must remember that communication skills take a while to improve. Since it is an ongoing process, we must be patient and persistent.

Chapter 8: Powerful Presentation

Presentations are a form of communication. Giving a brief, a sales pitch, an academic lecture, video conferencing, training sessions, orientations, wedding speeches, etc., are all fair examples of the different situations where we leverage the power of presentations to make an impact.

As listeners, we've experienced a fair share of dull and entertaining presentations. As speakers or presenters, we've felt a wide range of emotions as we stood before a gathering. Some of us have delivered presentations with élan, while others might have stumbled and fumbled through one and swore never to relive that nightmare.

Since presentations are an innate part of life, we need to understand the what's and why's, and how to overcome our fears and hesitancy and equip ourselves with a tool that will add to our effectiveness as communicators.

Broad Presentation Categories

#1 Informative

What was one of your earliest presentations? Show-and-tell at school, perhaps. And what did you do during show-and-tell? You presented something to your class and gave them information about it. Similarly, informative presentations are used to share knowledge, whether it is a lecture at a university, a training exercise at an office, awareness campaigns (think hygiene, fire safety, etc.), teachers presenting to parents, orientations, progress reports, etc., the application of presentations as a channel for information sharing is boundless.

#2 Persuasive

Remember the time you sought to convince your parents to fund your first car? Or even before, as a boy or girl scout when you went door-to-door persuading people to buy popcorn or cookies? An interview is a persuasion attempt (hire me). Imagine if you could appear for an interview armed with a multimedia presentation! A sales pitch to a prospective client, advocating for a new playground for local children or a community center, no smoking campaigns, etc. We use persuasive presentations when we want to present an idea and follow it up with supporting arguments and suggestions. Our goal here is to convince the audience to take an action—be it solving problems, making decisions, or perception changing.

Why are Presentations Necessary?

Presentations meet many needs. In a personal situation, you could mess up a presentation like a birthday or wedding or another congratulatory speech and not have many consequences to face. Apart from a little ridicule at the next family gathering, that is. However, in the business world, a presentation's success or failure could make or break a company. Let's quickly examine why presentations are necessary.

- There's nothing quite like meeting a client or a prospective client face-to-face. It is intimidating, yes. But to the experienced professional, it presents an opportunity like no other. A sales campaign can be watched and forgotten, but a powerful presentation is a chance to swing a nay toward a yay.

- Presentations allow the audience to absorb data quickly and glimpse over facts without all the noise in the form of speeches. It keeps their attention levels high, and it allows them to engage with the presenter—these all work in tandem to communicate your message to your audience with greater efficiency.

- Adaptability and flexibility are crucial, whether in a personal or professional situation. Presentations can be modified last minute; they can be online or offline; they can contain graphics or text or both; they address the unique needs of every person in the audience, and so much more.

- Barriers to effective communication within an organization can be removed through the formulation and use of formats or standard presentations. This provides a framework, consistency, and structure for how communication is handled within a company.

What are the Elements that Make a Bad Presentation?

Lack of presentation structure

Several thousand years ago, Aristotle made an observation that holds true even today—rational and logical arguments (logos) do not win debates. A speaker must devote an equal amount of energy stirring emotions (pathos) in their listeners and garner respect from their audience and establish credibility (ethos). Most speakers are unaware of how to structure their presentations. As a result, information and facts are all over the place. A hard-to-follow presentation will never sit well with the audience.

Speaker's inability to understand and assist the audience in their information processing needs

Processing information is never easy, even less so when our communication is complicated. When speakers struggle to deliver challenging or complex content, they often forget that their listeners will need help in decoding that content.

Failure to catch the audience's attention, inability to stir the correct emotions, inadequate comprehension, etc., all point toward lack of information processing.

Using the wrong stories

Humans have been telling stories from even before verbal communication developed. But where do these stories come from? Anywhere. Everywhere. As speakers, we need to pinpoint which stories will generate the correct or desired emotions in our audience. When there is a mismatch between our stories and our presentation's content, our audience's response will not be as desired. We will not connect with our listeners on a personal level. Worse still, our audience will not see us as interesting.

What are the Elements that Make a Good Presentation?

- **Content**

    Content refers to the information that is shared through your presentation. Since attention spans shrink year-on-year, the first element of a good presentation is ensuring that the information is limited to key facts. All additional details, features, tables, etc., should be shared in post-presentation documentation.

- **Structure**

    The content you need to share has to follow a specific structure or format to be logical and easy to follow. Like a story, a presentation's structure must have a starting point, a middle, and an end.

- **Packaging**

    A poorly packaged product rarely catches our attention. The same applies to presentations. The presented must be well prepared and should have the presentation skills necessary to ensure that the audience is captivated from the first word.

- **Necessity**

    Several mediums like reports, presentations, emails, conferences, etc., facilitate our need to communicate with large groups. Before jumping headfirst into the effort required for a presentation, we need to ascertain whether it is the most suitable medium for our audience's needs.

Presentation Hesitation

Public speaking is anxiety-producing, even if you've been giving presentations for years. The fear that we feel when we have to take the stage is what makes presentations difficult. Why are we so fearful? After all, we communicate daily. We persuade others every day. We present ourselves to individuals and groups regularly. Bargaining and negotiation are part of life. Even though we're seasoned when it comes to standing in front of an audience, we are still struck with fear and hesitancy when we have to give presentations.

Acknowledge the Barriers

Like anything else in life, presentations put us in a position where we'll be judged. We don't get a do-over, and we're under tremendous pressure to perform. The difference, however, is the immediacy of the judgment. For instance, if we write and send a poorly structured report or brief, we'll never see the look of disappointment or irritation when the recipient goes through the document. However, when we stand in front of an audience to present, we observe their reaction as it unfolds. A poor or undesirable response spurs us to stretch, to do whatever it takes to turn the presentation around, and we fumble more. The effects of rejection or poor audience reaction can have a profound impact on our confidence and self-esteem.

- We rarely overcome our fears. But we can manage them. We can channel them. And they can help us perform better. Figuring out why we're afraid and planning how to handle ourselves when the fear surfaces can make us better communicators. The first step is to recognize that it is perfectly normal to feel this anxiety and this fear.

- The next thing to remember is that this fear is both rational and irrational. It is rational in the sense that we're acutely aware of what happens during a presentation (audience judgment), and we're unwilling to risk that. It is irrational because communicating is something we do every day, yet we fear it when the scales increase. To counter this fear's effects, we must remember that writing and speaking have overlapping skills—skills that we've been practicing for years: structure, clarity, audience assessment, etc. By reminding yourself of this, you'll project greater confidence the next time you take center stage.

- Most of us are so floored by people who speak confidently and persuasively that it never occurs to us how many hours and hours they spent practicing. Communication is a practiced art. It comes naturally to all of us, and we observe and mimic others. However, just because we can communicate doesn't mean we're terrific at it. We cannot achieve efficiency in communication until we understand what makes communication effective and practice it.

- As odd as it may sound, one of the most important weapons of a skilled presenter is the ability to improvise. To be dynamic. And yes, even a skill like being dynamic and flexible needs to be practiced.

How to Handle the Fear?

Fear is natural. You don't have to squash it and pretend it doesn't exist. Being fearful is not a sign of weakness. How we handle our fear is what defines us.

Since fear is natural, our minds and bodies are conditioned to react to fear. Almost everyone understands what a fight-or-flight response is and why we respond to certain situations in certain ways. However, some situations call for a different reaction. When it comes to presentations, we must be counter intuitive. When we're under pressure to perform, we rarely make choices.

On the contrary, we tend to react. Since our actions aren't well-thought-out under stressful circumstances, they tend to cause chaos. This is another reason why fear is both rational and irrational. Our bodies are trying to protect us, but in the process, it makes the situation worse.

Counter the Effects of our Fight-or-Flight Response

Before we jump into what we can do to counter our instinctive reactions to stress, we need to understand what these reactions are and how they affect our abilities as presenters.

Let's divide our reactions into three broad categories.

Intellectual

We've all been in situations where we forget what it was that we were supposed to say. When we meet people and our mind draws a blank and we cannot recall their names. When we're looking straight at someone or something but we can't really focus. Think of the last time you were speaking to an audience. Did you find that there was a small, nagging voice in your head that kept telling you that you're boring? These are some of the intellectual reactions we have when we're under tremendous amounts of pressure. It is your body's way of trying to distance you from the activity causing the stress.

Verbal

Stuttering, fumbling through words, using a lot of filler words (er, um, actually, you know what, etc.) —when you find yourself desperately searching for something to say, that is your first cue that your body is responding to stress. We behave this way as we're trying to think superfast as we need to say something that makes us sound smart. But what we achieve is the complete opposite.

Physical

Physical responses are the worst, and perhaps the most noticeable of our reactions. Sweating profusely, tremors in our hands, dry mouth syndrome, moving your hands while you speak and being unable to stop the hand movement, shifty eyes, swaying back and forth, persistent nodding or head shaking, etc.—all of these make us acutely aware that we're displaying physical symptoms that others will pick up on.

Best Practices

Fear prevents us from being able to execute on multiple levels. These reactions, be it verbal, physical, or intellectual, become communication barriers. We focus on them instead of our task. For instance, if our attention shifts from our content, we cannot express ourselves. If we're spending energy trying to control trembling hands or swallowing to prevent that dry mouthfeel, we miss our audience's nonverbal or physical clues. As soon as we master our ability to control our fears, we can interact with our audience on a whole new level. We can create a mood and a tone that captures the audience's attention.

How do we go about mastering control over fear? Practice. We rehearse, and we practice our content. We put ourselves in a position that triggers our instinctive reactions, and we practice being ourselves while every cell in our bodies instructs us to do otherwise.

Another strategy that works wonderfully is to replace fear with a governed system—a formula. Presentations are, in essence, stories. If we approach them as a fright-inducing task, we'll never embrace it. We'll never move past the fear. To look at presentations from a different lens, something that we don't find intimidating, will help rewire our mindset. We can communicate with anyone. So why should this specific presentation scenario be any different? Is it because there are so many facts and figures, tables and charts, diagrams, notes, footnotes, etc., in our presentation?

All of the content that we deem necessary for our presentation can be delivered via email post the presentation. Horrifying thought, is it not? To stand on stage without a PowerPoint presentation lit up beside us. Or to not have that eerie green spreadsheet projected onto that wall from across investors and senior management.

At the bottom of it, we can deliver facts and figures through email. The human element is involved in a presentation because we bring something different to the presentation—turning content into a fascinating story.

Think about it.

Presentations are meant to be short, albeit they can seem like they go on forever. Regardless of their duration, the audience can only process and store a limited quantity of isolated information. So, packing your presentation with anything and everything, using the best, most recommended fonts, color-coded schemes, animations, etc., accomplishes little if your audience cannot retain that information.

Wouldn't it be better to send all that information via email for your audience to read and process at their pace? On the plus side, you won't have to brutally cut out information to keep your presentation short.

So, what do you do at a presentation?

You tell a story.

And for that story to be fascinating and memorable, you have to use a little science.

The EME

Why do people listen? Why do people remember? What helps people make decisions?

Ever wondered how you can work when a familiar song or tune is playing in the background but when something unfamiliar comes on, you can't focus on your task? Instead, you find yourself listening closely?

The three areas of the brain responsible for how we react to this scenario include: Emotions (why we listen), Memory (how we remember), and Empathy (how we make decisions).

Depending on the communication we're receiving, the EME either shuts down or it goes into overdrive. When the EME shuts down, we aren't listening, and we can't recall what was said. When the information is too complex, the EME gets overwhelmed and switches off. When you hear something that catches your attention, the EME becomes active, and listening and retention are natural by-products.

What is our goal during a presentation? To catch the audience's attention in a way that they listen and retain information.

How Do We Go About Engaging the EME?

Suspense. Creativity. Simplicity.

We use the SCS formula.

If you avoid predictability, employ surprises in your presentation, and keep your message simple (but not oversimple), your audiences' EME sections will be at their most active.

How do we use SCS to create interest? We use strategically placed content throughout our presentations, and whenever we're speaking.

Consider the following examples.

You're attending a seminar on the benefits of massage therapy. The presentation begins with facts. How many people get massages? What are the positive, therapeutic effects of massages? How do athletes benefit from massages? How do people with long-term pain conditions benefit from massages? You've lost interest.

Alternative: The presenter comes on stage and asks you a question. "Let's do a quick survey. How many here enjoy being touched by strangers?"

You were not expecting this. Your brain does a quick u-turn and you find yourself thinking, "What?" You take a moment to link the seminar topic to the opening statement and you are smiling.

"Can everyone say ahhh." Dentist convention.

"Can I have your wallets and checkbooks please?" Tax workshop.

"How would you like to be rich?" Investment presentation.

What are some of the other attention-grabbing sentences you can use?

- **Quotations**—as long as they're short. A quotation that's an entire paragraph long will be counterproductive.

- **References** to events, whether current or historical. Again, keep it short and if you feel you have to give context, then it's probably not the right attention-grabbing starter.

- **Personal anecdotes**

The secret to a great presentation—identify the underlying theme of your presentation and tie it all up in one opening sentence or question that confuses your audience and forces the EME section of their brain to think.

A good opening creates curiosity. It seems entirely unrelated for just that split second before the brain kicks in and you have a "eureka" moment.

You've probably heard this often enough. If you want a presentation to be interesting, start with a joke. Be humorous. Ask a question. And you've scripted it. You've practiced it. But when you're in front of a crowd or presenting over a web conference, the fear factor kicks in. Your normal tone changes. Your ability to tell a joke disappears. Everyone is looking at you and wondering, "Eh? Why was that funny?"

You break out in a cold sweat. Panic reflects in your expression. Your fight-or-flight response kicks in, and everything begins to go horribly wrong much faster as you react and try to fix the situation.

By using SCS and engaging the EME, you've got your icebreaker. You've created interest. You don't need to force humor. Let your content work for you. Not the other way around.

When we're interacting with others, we don't consciously think about what we're going to say. This is what makes natural conversation easy. This is why we don't feel pressure when we communicate with others. We don't have to divert our full attention to the other person or people.

By understanding how the brain functions and using that to our advantage, we can make our communication effective.

By engaging with the EME, you've maximized the possibility that your audience is going to remember whatever you've said.

Now that you have a great way to grab your listener's attention, what comes next? How do you follow up on that terrific SCS opening with something that will continue to engage with their EME?

A single sentence that summarizes your presentation. The one line that explains why you're presenting.

Here's an example:

> How would you like to be rich?
>
> <Pause for effect and for the EME to switch on.>
>
> In five years, you could be earning without working. By the time you retire, you could vacation anywhere without budget constraints.

The SCS opening is from the investment presentation. We know how investments work. You put up a certain amount of money monthly or annually, and it grows. But that's information everyone has. And if you repeat it in the presentation, you've bored the audience, and their EME has switched off.

However, once you drop something fantastic in front of your audience, you've got their complete attention.

What comes next?

Here is where you follow the general structure of a presentation. You begin not with your content but with the welcome, acknowledgment, and introduction.

> *How would you like to be rich?*
>
> *<Pause for effect and for the EME to switch on.>*
>
> *In five years, you could be earning without working. By the time you retire, you could vacation anywhere without budget constraints.*
>
> *<Pause for effect and for the EME to switch on.>*
>
> *Hello and welcome to... My name is...*
>
> *I want to take a moment to thank you for braving the snow to be with us today.*
>
> *I want to acknowledge the contributions of...*
>
> *I want to introduce...*

Acknowledgment, gratitude, and recognition are important to everyone, even the humblest amongst us. These are very powerful motivators. And in indulging these emotions, you've drawn your audience to you. You've closed that little gap of awkwardness—where everyone in the room turns from strangers to a community.

Be generous and smile. Be warm in your tone and expression. Remember the human element? If the objective were to create awareness about investing, a brochure would have sufficed. Why have a presentation instead? We interact because it helps us to connect with people, to influence, and to persuade them.

The Introduction

Think about all the times you've joined a new group. What's the first thing that happens? Everyone says hello and introduces themselves. Isn't that the moment where we all get stuck? What should we say? How do we introduce ourselves? Is it professional? Can we add personal details? How long should it be?

Introductions can be awkward. We're always wondering what we should say in an introduction. When in context with a presentation, think of introductions as a guide. An outline. It should briefly list the things that will be covered in the presentation, like the index of a book. You want to know what is in the book before you begin to read it. Similarly, in a presentation, people want to know what is being covered.

The introduction also serves a dual purpose. Parts of your presentation will invariably be of varying value to your listeners. While some may pay keen attention to a discussion on benefits, the section covering a roadmap might be more important to others. The introduction will key listeners into areas that are of value to them. Keep in mind that this is a journey your audience will be taking with you. Give them a feeling of security by telling them where they're headed.

The Body

We've talked about how surprises and unpredictability make for exciting content. So, the first issue we need to tackle in the main body of the presentation is learning to keep the audience surprised. While a roadmap (introduction) tells the audience what to expect, and the presentation's content needs to deliver just that, what we control is the "how."

Remember what we did with the EME? We shared the punchline first. That without context had our audience thinking, wondering, and smiling with the eureka moment. Now, as the story unfolds in the presentation body, the audience should be able to link that content back to the EME punchline. Toggle and juggle. Shift between facts and anecdotes. Facts encourage logical thinking while anecdotes stir up emotions. The two work in tandem to ensure retention. Move concepts around. Don't be rigid in a structure for the body of the presentation. Instead, learn keywords and then be flexible in the content you decide to share based on audience responses. If the audience seems interested, go into more detail. However, if they appear bored, eliminate that section of the presentation in favor of something that will engage their EME.

The Conclusion

The conclusion of a presentation should bring with it a sense of relief. You have arrived at the end of the experience. Or have you? Walking to the podium to give your presentation might have your stomach in knots, but the end is what most people usually dread. Why? Because it is here, after the conclusion, that the speaker must truly engage the audience with questions.

Questions can be intimidating. Most people feel as though they're being interrogated. They get overwhelmed or nervous, or both! They haven't prepared adequately and find themselves fumbling for something logical to say.

Change direction here. Instead of looking at the question and answer section of a presentation as the audience poking holes in your message, consider it a feedback opportunity. Remember what has been emphasized throughout—questions or feedback is part of the communication cycle. If you want to understand your presentation's impact on your audience, this is your golden opportunity. Use their questions as clues. Too many "how" questions mean you delivered just right—when your listeners want to know "how" to go about doing something, then it means they've accepted your idea.

Similarly, too many "what" or "why" questions would imply that your message wasn't quite as convincing. Your explanations could be what completes your audience's journey. It could be the one fact or one explanation that they need to accept your message.

Dynamic versus Static

What was the most boring thing about the last in-person presentation that you attended? Lack of activity, perhaps? A monotone that lulled you to sleep? A presentation slide that you read several times over, and it still didn't change?

Static is boring.

Just as content needs to be juggled, so does a speaker's tone and position. Most speakers feel "safe" behind a podium, like a game of hide-and-seek with a child. You can see them. But they feel invisible just because they can't see you.

Speakers who are acutely aware of the "fear" factor and the fight-or-flight response become static. Perhaps hand trembling is a physical indication of their discomfort, and so they keep their hands flat on the podium. If their intellectual stress-induced response is to draw a blank, they feel it's safer to read from a script or the slides on the screen. They don't make eye contact with the audience. As a result, the presentation becomes dull.

The easiest way to infuse energy into a room full of people is to be energetic. You cannot achieve that by being static. Move around. A series of (controlled) hand movements will disguise the hand trembling. Purposeful pacing might channel your anxiety. It might clear your mind and return your focus.

When a speaker exudes confidence, we automatically tend to lend their message a certain degree of credibility. You've structured your speech, added a few surprises and anecdotes, memorized keywords, and put together the perfect EME punchline. What else can you do to earn credibility?

Use your body language. Confidence comes not just from our tone when we speak. It can be seen in our nonverbal cues. When you rehearse your speech, remember to also check your body language for ambiguity. Stand not in front of a tiny mirror but a full-length one. Observe what your hands are doing. See which way your torso is angled. Are your shoulders drooping? Do you tend to rub your chin or frown when you're stressed? Make a note of which part of the presentation triggers that body language and address it.

Your nonverbal cues are a powerful communication medium. Remember that the fight-or-flight response is not just verbal or intellectual. It's also physical. Acknowledge that response. Replace unintended gestures with intentional ones. If you are conscious of too many hand gestures, stand beside the podium with one hand on it, not both. If you tend to shrink away from the audience, make a conscious effort to angle your torso toward them.

Chapter 9 Part 1: Communication Strategies for a Virtual Age

What is Virtual Communication?

Virtual communication is the use of technology as a medium to aid in the interaction process between individuals or teams of people that are not physically present in the same space. The person you are speaking with could be in the next room, or a different office floor, the building next door, or even in a different country. Virtual communication is a broad category that would include everything from a phone call to a text message, video conferencing to chat messengers, e-training and email, and so much more. Technology is so ingrained into our lives that we use virtual communication in all walks of our life.

The current COVID pandemic has changed the way we communicate, work, network, and collaborate personally and professionally. Almost all in-office teams were forced to change into virtual teams, and the world saw an influx of remote workers on a never-seen-before scale. Businesses were forced to adapt. Who wouldn't when confronting a sink-or-swim situation?

Virtual communication became the new norm, or did it? Think about real time data, instant news updates, information sharing across the globe with the push of a button. We've been communicating virtually for decades; now we just need to strategize differently to reap its benefits.

What are Some of the Advantages of Virtual Teams and Virtual Communication?

Any business that endeavored to establish a presence beyond local borders is already familiar with the advantages (and challenges) of virtual communication. These range from increased productivity to reduced business costs, speed, increased convenience, a better work-life balance, etc. Let's have a look at these in greater detail.

Time Saving and Convenient

Gone are the days when the commute to office took an hour (or a few hours) each way. No more rushing to catch trains and buses, no more being jostled around by never-ending swarms of people. Working from the comforts of home or a home office means not having to brave the cold or heat or pollution. The time you save on commuting on a daily basis can now be spent catching up with family, pursuing a hobby, giving time and attention to a child or a spouse. Since this time saving factor contributes to better work-life balance, employees will be happier and that will lead to an increase in productivity.

Cost-effective

Most businesses include transport or fuel compensation in their employees' packages. With a larger part of the workforce working remotely, there is a dramatic reduction in operational costs of employees.

Businesses that employ virtual teams in countries where the purchasing power of currencies like the Dollar or Euro or Pound is lower will save a lot on employee costs.

Remote working options also eliminate the need to create space for a growing pool of employees. Benefits are also seen in the form of reduced utility costs and food/beverage expenses.

Speed

In a fast-paced world, slow just doesn't cut it. And virtual communication means everyone is just a click away.

Harness Talent from Anywhere

When having a virtual team was a choice, businesses could choose to recruit locally. In most countries, hiring from an international pool meant providing supporting and lengthy explanations to governments. Now that remote employment is a necessity, even for local hires, it has opened businesses to the possibility of recruiting talent from across the globe. And without the burden of sponsoring immigrants, having a virtual team means businesses and people have access to opportunities like never before.

24/7

A significant advantage of a globally distributed team (at least for the IT and services industry) is that business never has to stop. Because of the time zone difference, when one team switches off, another can take its place. Work continues round-the-clock, a surefire way for companies to reduce their turn-around-time for projects and respond to client communication quicker.

Ease of Maintaining Records

Virtual communication enables individuals and organizations to maintain records with the push of a button. Conducting a training session or an important web meeting? Click that little red button and everything is recorded for you. Upload that to your company's internal portal and it's available to all employees. Today, companies can even monitor employee attention levels during online events. The idea is not to snoop on employees, but to better understand how to make online events more efficient and engaging.

What are Some of the Disadvantages of Virtual Teams and Virtual Communication?

Understanding disadvantages of virtual communication and virtual teams will help businesses to strategize on how best to communicate effectively virtually.

Technical Problems

Virtual communication relies on power, software, machines, and the Internet, all of which can disconnect or malfunction at any time. This impacts ongoing or scheduled virtual communication efforts.

Additional Responsibilities and Less Control

Having a work-from-home team makes it challenging to monitor productivity levels. A tremendous amount of trust needs to be extended to employees, and companies that have suffered because of lower productivity levels will micro-monitor and micro-manage. Full integration and appropriate management of remote workers then become additional responsibilities for managers and team leaders.

Cross-Cultural Differences

When virtual teams interact, cross-cultural differences become highly noticeable. Considering different global communication styles and varied intercultural working practices, virtual communication between cross-cultural teams can lead to conflicts.

An understanding of cultural variables and their effect is required for businesses to navigate through these challenges and make virtual communication more effective.

Communication Mistakes in Virtual Communication and In-person Communication

A little thinking exercise:

- How often do you get bored during office or virtual meetings?

- Do you find yourself navigating from a web conference or meeting to other sites?

- How often do you attentively sit through a presentation (as opposed to sourcing the slides and looking over them later)?

The three most common mistakes people make during both in-person meetings, as well as virtual communication, include speaking in third person, using formal language, and providing too many details.

Speaking in Third Person

Consider the following examples:

1. When we work late or when we are highly stressed, we often find ourselves reaching out for a convenient snack. We consume the snack without thought to its health quotient, or lack of. The calories add up. It is important for people to pay attention to their choices and identify where they are consuming these additional calories.

2. For a week, each time that I stepped in front of my fridge, I made a conscious effort to avoid anything that might have sugar, natural as well as artificial. By the end of that week, I found that I lost a few pounds.

The first example is written in third person narrative. It sounds boring. It feels like advice. Anyone reading or listening to such communication will tune out after the first few minutes. The second example, however, would catch most people's attention. It uses the "I" or first-person narrative. It sounds more convincing. No matter how flawed an argument or premise, the minute someone says they tried it and it worked for them, we're more inclined to believe it.

The next time you find yourself nodding alongside an infomercial, focus on which narrative style it follows. How soon after it started did you find yourself convinced by it? Even if the results or premise remain unproven, do you find yourself excited about trying it? Now apply this to a presentation or virtual meeting and see how differently your audience behaves.

Using Formal Language

Another mistake that most people make during meetings, in-person as well as virtual, is the extensive use of formal language. One of the earlier chapters covered barriers to effective communication, and one of these was complexity of the sender's message. Overly formal language can sound pretentious. It also makes it hard to identify and absorb the sender's message.

Consider the following examples:

- Good morning. This is our fifth series in the previously outlined e-training module. I thank you all for taking the time to be here today.

- My mom called the other day, and as she spoke about her difficulty with meal planning, I wondered if an app that rotates meal options might help remove some of her stress.

Which of the two made you yawn? Did you zone out? Skip the sentences entirely? Whether in person or in virtual meetings, the language used can make or break the audience's experience.

Too Many Details

Consider the following example:

A few weeks ago, I decided to surprise my partner with a romantic meal. I scoured the fanciest restaurants in our neighborhood. The ambience had to be perfect, you see. And I finally found a restaurant that had a rooftop setup. The building where the restaurant leased space was on a corner side property that ran parallel to the river. The entire rooftop space was surrounded by potted palm trees wrapped in those little Christmas tree sort of lights. Since the building the restaurant was located in was taller than its surrounding counterparts, I had a clear view of the river. As I went in the evening, I could see the reflection of the nearby lights in the water. It was quite lovely, you see.

What if I just said this?

Imagine the perfect romantic dinner for two.

That's what I arranged for my partner as a birthday surprise.

Need I say more?

Addressing Preconceived Notions

Most people will swear by the effectiveness of in-person communication. And why not? We've been doing it all our lives. Let's quickly cover some of the advantages of in-person interaction.

- In-person interaction allows people to feed off each other's ideas.

- Face-to-face conversations can lead to continuing dialogue.

- It promotes relationships.

- It instills trust and builds transparency.

- Greater range of nonverbal cues.

- It helps create an atmosphere of equality.

- It is immediate.

But is it all good? Are there no downsides to in-person interaction? Let's quickly list some disadvantages of in-person communication.

- It is ineffective when many people are involved as communication is hindered.

- It is costly especially in a business context. Think of the resources it takes especially if the team is geographically placed.

- Planning becomes challenging as everyone's schedule needs to be considered.

- Post meeting/interaction documentation.

- Personality clashes become more glaring and can quickly spin out of control, leading to a greater likelihood of conflict.

What about Virtual Communication?

Advantages of Virtual Communication

- Easier to voice concerns or raise questions (especially in written communication).

- Speed and time factors.

- Globalization is not just a fancy term.

- Increased productivity.

- Shorter meeting spans.

- Allows people time to think and formulate their responses, reduces possibilities of impulse replies.

- Eliminates post interaction/meeting/workshop documentation.

- Meeting logistics and associated expenses are not a concern.

- Suitable for all communication styles, personalities, learning preferences.

Disadvantages of Virtual Communication

- Delay in decision making (takes a while to get input from all participants and stakeholders).

- Limited access to nonverbal cues.

- Technical requirements and associated issues.

That merits the question, is in-person communication better than virtual? What about the notion that people feel more involved and part of an organization when in the same physical space? Does the "tribe" feeling, or sentiment, not develop when people are part of virtual teams?

Heard of MMORPG games? A massively multiplayer online role-playing game, popularly referred to as MMORPG, is a story driven video game in which multiple players interact with each other while taking on the persona of a character in the fantasy virtual world.

They have people banding together in teams, tribes, and groups, and working together. How many of them even know each other's real names? Is it possible to read body language or other nonverbal cues? Most don't even speak the same language, beyond a few basic words, and yet they bridge the language barrier effortlessly.

So, if virtual communication has brought the world together via MMORPG's, why are most people so against it in a business context?

Effectiveness in Virtual Communication

After months and months of virtual communication with your team, efficiency is a given. Or is it? What are the mistakes people make while communicating through virtual channels? And how can we make these channels more effective? What are some of the ways through which we can enhance overall virtual performance?

While we may be adept at virtual communication in our social life, and perhaps we're masters of sending emails and text messages while taking a bus or riding the train, are we quite as comfortable and efficient when it comes to other forms of virtual communication?

As with any form of communication, and with anything new that we bring into our lives, virtual communication takes more effort. It requires conscious thought.

What to Avoid

When we are annoyed with someone over something they said or did, we have the tendency to attack the person rather than the behavior. When someone cuts you off in traffic, we are likely to think, "He is rude and doesn't deserve a license!" When someone expresses a need for something, instead of empathizing, don't we think, "Isn't she selfish?" or "Who does she think she is? How could she expect that? Isn't she entitled?"

However, when we catch ourselves making mistakes, we're more forgiving. We tend to justify our words and actions based on circumstances.

This tendency needs to be checked during virtual communication because we have fewer nonverbal cues to rely on. While we will continue to make attributional errors anyway, virtual communication's limitations intensify this challenge. We can't see facial expressions very well, tones are harder to judge, body language not covered in a screen or a call cannot be factored in how we decode the intent of the communication—and these are just a few examples.

Attaching meaning to actions and messages, jumping to conclusions, indulging in conjecture—each of these barriers to effective communication applies to virtual communication as well. What is your first thought when someone doesn't turn on their camera during a video conference? Are you more likely to believe that person is considerate because their familial situation might distract everyone in the meeting? Or that they are camera shy or perhaps too lazy to dress appropriately for a camera-based meeting? When someone is late, how likely are we to think they are tardy rather than they had internet issues?

Addressing Attribution Bias

How can we make everyone feel involved and equally valued?

People Need Space

Adjusting to working styles and conditions, reducing distractions, setting boundaries for family members to follow, etc., is causing people to stress more. Tensions are higher, and so is the likelihood of conflict. Be human. Make accommodations. Be more understanding. For instance, instead of being rigid about punctuality when starting virtual meetings, keep the first few minutes for social interaction. That will give people with technical or other issues grace period. Not all meetings have to be the on-camera kind. Some can be off-camera as well.

Empathy Builds Relationships

Repetitive advice, perhaps. But essential. Cognitive and emotional empathy take precedence in uncertain times. Humans are social creatures. We crave connections.

Working remotely can make people feel isolated. Close-knit teams are more invested in each other's success. Take some time for personal interactions. Celebrate virtually when projects are completed. Keep tabs on birthdays and anniversaries. Have a coffee meet or beer get together. Build rapport. The empathy, compassion, and forgiveness you demonstrate will help build relationships.

Be Respectful, Professional, and Prepared

It is easy to forget that behind every avatar is a real person. You see a nameless, faceless icon representing a team member but forget that they deserve the same respect and courtesies you'd offer then in an in-person meeting. Check this behavior to maintain trust, team cohesiveness, and engagement.

Don't let good habits slide. It is true that your team isn't in the same physical space as you, but that doesn't mean you can read from a note on your computer. Prepare just like you would for an in-office meeting. It doesn't mean you can play games during a session and catch up with slides and emails later. It makes you a passive participant in conferences, and it doesn't go unnoticed. Dress appropriately. While it's acceptable to wear a T-shirt rather than a collared shirt, it doesn't reflect well on you to have a week-long stubble and a food-stained shirt. Be professional. Who knows? Taking a shower, dressing well, fussing over your appearance—all these routine habits can pull you out of any funk you might be feeling from working remotely.

Ask Questions

The quiet, shy, keep-to-themselves kind of team members are easily overlooked in a non-virtual office environment. They aren't the kind to be front and center in a virtual meeting. Like all other team members, they will have challenges and need to know that support and help are available. How can anyone feel like they're part of a team if there is no concern? Ask questions—check-in without being invasive. Let them know they are part of the team. Let them know that they haven't been forgotten.

Be Forgiving

Mistakes are commonplace in any environment, be it social or professional. Why should remote employees be expected to be perfect? Understand that team members are adjusting to a new work environment, and it's probably not as productive, especially if the person is a social butterfly and needs constant interaction with team members. How many all-nighters can people pull without feeling anxiety? Wouldn't that affect their productivity levels? Be attuned to performance-related issues and identify which team member needs help. Give feedback. Offer support. Be forgiving.

Recognition

Just because we communicate virtually or have virtual teams doesn't mean that we allow the distance or the remote working situation to prevent us from celebrating achievements. Most employees crave recognition. And one of the ways organizations can boost morale and make everyone feel valued is to continue recognizing efforts. The perfect way to start a meeting is with an appreciative note about someone's hard work or key milestones. Recognition in front of peers is a fantastic way to earn people's loyalty.

A few tips for virtual team communication:

- Video and voice-only conference call groups should have a small number of attendees. Dialogue, whether in person or virtually, is not supported when participant numbers are overwhelming.

- Just as we would handle conflict or difficult conversations in private, one-on-one issues should be addressed offline, and definitely not during conferences or meetings.

- Personalization is important. Call remote members by their names.

- Not every meeting should be professional. Make time to have quick, personal conversations.

Showing interest and providing support makes people feel valued.

- If someone is upset or sends a bitter mail, be proactive. Call them. Don't write. And don't delay your response.

- Using instant messaging makes remote team members feel like a part of the group.

- Agree to regular meetings, but keep non-work communication channels open.

Strategies for Positive Difficult Conversations and How to Make People Feel Valued and Heard

Uncomfortable conversations are unenviable responsibilities, whether in a social or professional context. They rarely start pleasantly, and they don't end on a positive note. If not handled delicately enough, senior team members often criticize the person rather than address the behavior.

One of the challenges of connecting virtually is that it makes these difficult conversations more challenging. So, what is the best way to have these conversations? How do you avoid putting the other person on the defensive?

Here's a four-step process (the 4 A's) to address sensitive issues with a virtual team. The best part? We can adapt this strategy to the real world, as well.

Address

Now, this is a two-part step.

1. Conversations in third person narrative aren't particularly exciting. However, difficult conversations in third person narrative prevent the other person from feeling as though they're being isolated and attacked. It's the first step in preventing them from getting defensive from the beginning of the conversation.

2. Address a pattern. Not a behavior. Certainly not the person.

So, begin the conversation with something along the lines of, "We've seen a lot of late submissions lately." You're making a statement here. You're not questioning. If the person is guilty of late submissions, their first response will be to accept responsibility and provide an explanation. "Yes, I know, but it couldn't be helped because..."

Admit

No one is perfect. Least of all, the person leading the difficult conversation. But have you ever heard or seen a senior member admit to making mistakes? People are less likely to be honest with you if you portray yourself as flawless. After all, how can you relate to someone if you haven't had similar experiences? Be human. Admit to your shortcomings, even if it is stretching the truth a bit.

A continuation of your earlier sentence would take the conversation further. "We've seen a lot of late submissions lately. I know I have missed a few key deliveries. I feel like I'm juggling too much."

With something that simple, you've taken the focus off that person. You've just turned a difficult conversation into an honest discussion.

Assess

You began the difficult conversation by stating a pattern. You've taken responsibility. You've provided a perfectly plausible reason for why you messed up. By now, the other person should feel as though they can trust you and be honest with you. Once you've reached this stage, hand control to them. Ask them for their assessment. For their opinion. This is the crucial stage where they'll feel "heard."

Ask

Once you have the input, you need to understand the what-and-why of the difficult behavior; "ask" the other person for a solution. No one likes to be "told."

"The consequences would be terrible if..." a conversation that begins like that is going to end terribly. It works better if you say something like "What do you think we can do? Is there something we can try for a month and see if it is a more suitable alternative?"

Subtle threats, serious consequences, ultimatums just don't give the desired outcome. We want the discussion to result in something positive. By allowing the other person to come up with a situation and putting a time frame on it, they won't feel backed into a corner. They won't feel as though there will be undesirable consequences.

This is how you sensitively address a difficult conversation and get a positive outcome.

Effective and Impactful Meetings

How to Structure a Highly Effective Meeting

Meetings should be fun, right? Isn't it a refreshing change from clacking away at a keyboard in isolation? Meetings are an excellent way to get involved with problems and be part of the solution, no? But how many of us actually welcome meetings, in-person or virtual?

Meetings can be a drag. People come, and people go. Everyone sits in their favorite corners of the room. The energy in the room is tense rather than relaxed. Sometimes people have no idea what they're doing there or why they were called. Uncertainty looms. The dread truly sets in when people start talking. There's more talking and more talking. There are presentations and more talking. How many times have you attended a meeting and felt it was productive?

Are virtual meetings the same as in-person meetings? You schedule time off work, lecture your spouse or children about not interrupting you. In the last meeting, your child ran up to you and started bawling, snot dripping everywhere. You've never felt more unprofessional in your career, right?

But what if there was a way to make virtual meetings fun and effective?

Let's start with the obvious—have an agenda.

Here's the catch—apply rules to increase the effectiveness of your agenda.

Here's how.

Set a clear purpose. It's not a clear purpose for the meeting. You've already done that. It's a clear purpose for every person attending. Make sure you spend time contacting each attendee and sharing with them why they've been asked to attend and what is expected from them in terms of participation. This helps in several ways:

a) You've eliminated uncertainty. Everyone knows why they're there.

b) Since everyone is pitching in, they'll pay more attention. Each person will wait for their cue to start speaking. This will keep them from switching off. It will increase the likelihood that they'll listen attentively.

Unreasonable time. When did a meeting ever end on time? When did people speak only for the duration they were supposed to? When planning a meeting, factor in these issues. When you share the agenda with specific people who have to speak, allot them speaking time. If you know their report will take 10 minutes to share, give them 5 minutes. It's an unreasonable amount of time.

But once they know when they're talking, and how much time they have, they're going to plan better. During the meeting, that unreasonable time constraint will force them to utilize their time effectively.

Homework. Include potential for homework in the agenda that you share pre-meeting. This forces everyone attending to work on areas that need addressal. It makes a meeting productive because everyone knows what they're supposed to do after.

What Else Makes a Meeting Effective?

Rules for responding and for communicating also add to the effectiveness of teams and meetings. When people know what is expected of them and how they are to deliver it, that meeting becomes efficient. These rules can be simple. For instance, inform everyone that after a topic has concluded, they need to agree or disagree and provide a brief explanation. Another rule could be that the person introducing a specific idea needs to discuss its merits and introduce why it doesn't work.

While different teams and meetings will require different sets of rules, what makes rule-keeping efficient is that everyone agrees to them. Understanding how a meeting is to run and setting the engagement rules are crucial precursors that determine a meeting's effectiveness.

A terrible meeting environment is one where people are not engaged. In-person meetings can kick off like that. People enter the designated room, take their seats, and busy themselves on their phones or laptops. Pre-meeting engagement is nonexistent. Everyone is eventually prompted to say hi, and then the awkwardness returns. This is mirrored in virtual meetings as well. People log into the meeting and go about their business while they wait for all attendees to gather. No one speaks with each other. There is no catching up, no light banter, nothing.

Introducing an activity a few minutes before the meeting's official start will counter this awkwardness. Using icebreakers is also a great way to get virtual teams to speak with each other. Rapport building activities also set the tone for how the group will communicate as the meeting progresses.

Create a dynamic environment with your very first slide. Put a question in it and instructions. Ask the participants to begin work as soon as they enter the meeting. Get them involved by asking them to address other participants' questions.

As the meeting progresses, people tend to get stiff. They get bored and lose interest. Some meetings just have to be technical and cannot have fun elements. How do you keep people interested? How can you raise energy levels?

The **first step** is to ask rhetorical questions. Even if people zone out while someone else is speaking, a question catches them off-guard. They don't know it's rhetorical, and they automatically pay attention. As soon as they re-enter the conversation, they become active participants.

The **second step** is to time your rhetorical questions. As soon as a topic or idea has ended, position a few rhetorical questions. Not only does it get the audience thinking, but it also re-engages them.

As a **third step**, include the potential for some kind of activity. It could be something as simple as raising hands to show agreement. It could be as involved as breaking the audience into groups and giving them a quick collaborative task. It is essential to include that there must be some sort of deliverable from the task—a YouTube video on a topic that demonstrates the advantages of the issue under discussion, for instance.

Another way we can engage people is with discussion questions. Again, there must be a deliverable. It's counterproductive to say, "Listen, I want you to research this topic." If the deliverable is post-meeting, then the person tasked with the research has no incentive to be active in that moment. However, if the deliverable is within minutes of the task being assigned, accompanied with the understanding that it's the first discussion and no "in-depth preparation" is needed, you'll stir everyone into an active state.

Chapter 9 Part 2: What In-person Communication Principles and Techniques Can We Apply to Virtual Teams?

As COVID forced the world to transition to remote work, our dependency on virtual communication increased. To meet these needs, collaborative technologies—each offering something fantastic—saturated the market. This has led to a tremendous amount of confusion as most people and companies assume that the more sophisticated the tool, the more effective it will make virtual communication. However, research has shown that it is not the technology that makes communication effective. It is the people using the technology.

When working with virtual teams, it is prudent to reach beyond emails, texts, discussion forums, and document or project management systems. If possible, schedule at least one or two events with your virtual team.

Here's an example of how:

A virtual water cooler. You know how people at an office band in the lunchroom or at the nearest water faucet or cooler? Some of your colleagues might even use their break to walk to the closest coffee shop or step out for a smoke.

Why do people do that? Why do they move away from their desks and out of range of their seniors or managers? Do they really need to stretch their legs, or is something else motivating them to get this "space?"

In the real world, an office environment is a busy one. Everyone might be working. But there's a lot of chit chat. A lot of gossip. A lot of venting. People moving around. The convenience of being right next to someone with whom you share a team culture, a unique communication code, even a team language encourages interaction.

This convenience is missing from a virtual team. So how do you go about recreating this? How do you encourage this kind of gossip station?

You create a virtual water cooler. It's a safe place to convene—no managers or seniors allowed. Do a quick survey within the group for which chat or messaging tool is favored and create a group. Add people to the group and elect a few moderators. Everyone needs to be sworn to secrecy—it will be unethical and to one's own detriment to take screenshots of conversations. And then use that space to encourage water-cooler-level interaction.

Make it safe for juniors to ask questions without being judged.

What happens if the team is too unfamiliar with each other and the chatroom doesn't take off as it should?

Have a moderator or administrator add a daily task. No. It's not work.

Schedule events. How many times did the in-office team leave for post-work drinks? Organize such an event virtually. Select a time when most of the group is available or has the highest likelihood of being available (post-dinner, Sunday lunch, etc.) and meet at that time. Have something whacky planned as an icebreaker. Virtual Pictionary? Virtual truth or dare? Virtual beer-o-clock? Virtual chess tournament?

Connecting through communication is one of the most profound ways in which you can improve workplace relationships and invite success in your career.

When communicating virtually, all of the same in-person communication techniques are applicable. However, we must add a layer of mindfulness and thoughtfulness. After all, no matter how we communicate, as message senders, we need to think of the recipient and be conscious of how they will perceive our messages. This is equally, if not more important, when we communicate virtually.

To extend this courtesy to our peers and seniors, we simply need to be mindful about whether or not they're comfortable with virtual communication. This matters because even though the world is growing more dependent on virtual communication, not everyone is comfortable communicating this way.

What are some of the conditions that we need to keep in mind?

- Ask if your recipient is comfortable communicating via e-mail, phone call, text, or camera-based web calls and conferences.

- If communicating with someone in another time zone, check on their day or night before sending your communication. Alternatively, ask them if a proposed time for a meeting suits them before finalizing and sharing the time.

- When communicating virtually in writing, revise your message and check for tone.

- Most companies have guidelines for virtual communications to maintain confidentiality and protect proprietary information. Learn what (if any) those boundaries are and follow them.

One of the reasons why communication with a virtual team becomes challenging is that we are unfamiliar with norms, languages, styles, and customs.

Consider the following issues:

Language differences - While geographically dispersed teams may speak or communicate with each other in one language, English, for instance, may not be everyone's first language. As such, people's fluency levels vary. They may not understand idioms or local slang, for example.

Gestures differ - What is considered a peace sign in the US, is offensive in the UK. Touching heads is regarded as a sign of affection in most countries, but it's an offensive action in Thailand. A "rock on" sign flashed at a man in Italy would imply that his wife is cheating on him. Pointing with your index finger can offend a Malaysian. It only takes a few moments to quickly research what is considered offensive or polite in the country where your virtual counterparts are based. And that one moment of consideration could build a lifetime of rapport and trust.

What is considered safe?

- Keep your communication simple so that it doesn't overwhelm any team member.

- Speak slowly. When we're nervous or anxious, we tend to speak faster. This increases the chances of confusion and misinterpretation.

- Smile. Since nonverbal cues are hard to identify and decode in virtual communication, smiling ensures that there are fewer chances of misinterpretations. You'll also appear warm, approachable, and likable.

- Don't read "between the lines" in any form of written communication, be it email or text. Remind yourself that you don't know the sender on a personal level and hence, should not conjecture or speculate. When in doubt, ask clarifying questions instead.

Which communication tool to use?

Advances in technology that brought us into the digital era (smartphones, desktops, laptops, tablets) saw a surge in the use of communication channels like basic e-mail, online texts, forums, conference, or video calls, etc. Today, some 40 years later, our choices have ballooned exponentially. Aside from all the basic channels receiving constant upgrades and sophistication, we've got new providers (it's not just Microsoft or AOL anymore); several other channels or tools have mushroomed as well, ranging from dozens of options for social networks, forums, messenger apps, platforms like Slack, Zoom, Microsoft Teams, etc. Is it a wonder that we're all confused about which tool to use and for which purpose?

When considering a virtual meeting, you need to consider all the options that your organization uses, and then identify which one will suit your needs perfectly. Don't be that person that clicks "video call" for everything.

Let's go over some basic virtual communication challenges and how they can be addressed with the tools and platforms available.

Poor Communication

Communication doesn't always mean an exchange of messages, verbal or otherwise. When working remotely, most people feel isolated.

Consider these scenarios:

> **In-office**: You had the first meeting. You've explained tasks to everyone. Everyone returns to their desk, and the chatter begins. Every tea or coffee break, every trip to the bathroom, every smoke walk, etc., the entire office floor is like a busy bazaar. Even if everyone is quiet, it's noisy. All the phones ringing, the people coming and going, the whir of machines like printers, tapping of fingers or feet, pens and pencils hitting the floor, snack packets being ripped open, smells everywhere. All

you have to do is look up from your screen and know that you aren't alone. If you're working late, people will sympathize with you on their way out, and some might even extend help. It's easy to feel like a part of your team.

Virtual: You had the first meeting. You've explained tasks to everyone. The end of the week swings past, and you haven't spoken with anyone from your team. When you reach out, the feedback you receive is that most people's morale is low, and they cite poor communication as the leading factor.

People crave communication, and a lack of informal face-to-face interaction can impact team cohesiveness. Video conferences are perfect for enhancing day-to-day interactions. It aids in the building of trust and strengthening team communication bonds. Create that virtual water cooler and watch your team come alive. You can also boost interaction by setting one-on-one time between managers and employees. They will prove incredibly beneficial when employees need to discuss goal setting, frustrations, or blockers, and more.

Trust

When people work virtually, mistrust often builds between team members. This becomes a significant barrier in terms of communication and management of virtual teams. Since members rarely work during the same hours, they cannot see what others are doing. Responses are slow and act as an impediment to progress. Set rules of engagement so that everyone knows what the appropriate response times ought to be. Set one medium of communication (like instant messenger) so that it's easier to reach out to someone. Use an online platform to help with scheduling and tracking of task updates so that everyone can see what everyone else is doing. Even if they're not working the same hours, just seeing that work getting done is enough to instill trust. Make virtual communication a source of joy.

Additional suggestions for engagement rules:

- Conference calls are best when you do not need to share images. If it's just a weekly or bi-weekly team catch up, a discussion regarding tasks, etc., then a conference call will suit your requirements.

- Since conference calls typically include many people, the sheer number becomes a barrier to communication as everyone is struggling to give their input and be heard.

- Documents should only be shared in a conference call if they're easy to navigate. It is counterproductive to email your team a 40-page document and during the call, ask them to flip to page 20 and then wait 5 minutes for everyone to navigate. Quick and easy tasks over a conference call will make them less painful for everyone.

- Send documents by e-mail and give people time to familiarize themselves with the content before introducing it in a conference, especially if anyone in the conference is unfamiliar with the language.

- Webinars are best suited for when slides or images need to be shared, and everyone needs to see them simultaneously.

- For all virtual communication, ensure that every team member has the right equipment and connectivity. Virtual communication that is not adequately supported becomes a pain point if people can't hear each other, can't see images, need hours to buffer, etc.

- Be flexible and proactive; when technology becomes a barrier, don't be afraid to end a meeting. Reschedule and send the reading material in advance. At the next meeting, keep it short using tips to make virtual meetings more effective.

Cross Cultural Training

Virtual teams often include people from different ethnic groups—each with complex cultural norms. When customs, habits, values, etc., become a source of conflict, it is wise to have short cultural training sessions so that all team members are aware of what is causing the friction and what they can do to avoid it.

Consistency

Communication and information sharing tools are a necessity as such platforms simplify our daily tasks and facilitate interaction. However, they can do more harm than good if everyone is not consistent. For instance, if file-sharing happens via various hosting sites, then there will be utter confusion about where to find documents or other content. Meetings are held, and the post-meeting documentation creation is automatic. But does your team know where to locate those files? Everyone should work from the same platform to avoid chaos and fragmented understanding.

Feedback

Even when everything seems to be working perfectly on the surface, there could be undercurrents of dissatisfaction. Feedback is a powerful tool which managers or team leaders can use to identify obstacles and streamline the process and communication protocols. Listening to your team is essential but acting on that feedback is critical to team cohesiveness.

The incorrect approach to managing virtual teams can result in friction. However, a few adjustments to communication styles and channels, along with management of remote employees, can improve morale and increase productivity.

www.ingramcontent.com/pod-product-compliance
Lightning Source LLC
Chambersburg PA
CBHW071430070526
44578CB00001B/52